EXTRAORDINARY
MOMENTS
WITH GOD

Sharon Jaynes

HARVEST HOUSE PUBLISHERS

EUGENE, OREGON

EXTRAORDINARY MOMENTS WITH GOD

Copyright © 2008 by Sharon Jaynes
Published by Harvest House Publishers
Eugene, Oregon 97402
www.harvesthousepublishers.com

Library of Congress Cataloging-in-Publication Data

Jaynes, Sharon.
  Extraordinary moments with God / Sharon Jaynes.
   p.cm
  ISBN-13: 978-0-7369-2252-4
  ISBN-10: 0-7369-2252-0
  1. Devotional literature. 2. Meditations. I. Title.
BV4832.3.J39 2008
242'.5—dc22

                                                    2008001009

Printed in China

08 09 10 11 12 13 14 15 16 / RDS-NISK / 10 9 8 7 6 5 4 3

This book is dedicated to my son, Steven.

*One of my most extraordinary moments with God
was when you were placed in my arms
in the delivery room.*

What a joy it is to be your mom.

I love you…more.

A Word to the Reader

How do ordinary days become filled with extraordinary moments? By listening to God's still, small voice and seeing His fingerprints on the pages of our lives. Just as God spoke to the uneducated fisherman, the woman at the well, and the shepherds in the field, He continues to speak to ordinary men and women in the middle of their busy days. All day long God speaks to us through the Bible, prayer, creation, nature, circumstances, and people who cross our paths. The key is recognizing the gentle nudge, detecting God's voice, and turning aside from the busyness to see the burning bushes in our own backyards.

Join me now as we dust for God's fingerprints on the pages of our lives to discover extraordinary moments with Him.

1

Someone's Knocking

*Here I am! I stand at the door and knock. If
anyone hears my voice and opens the door, I will
come in and eat with him, and he with me.*

REVELATION 3:20

When I was a little girl I sat in a sparsely decorated Sunday school room and mused over
a solitary picture of Jesus that hung on a stark-white
wall. In this picture Jesus stood peacefully knocking
at someone's door. I can remember wondering, *Why
is He knocking? Why doesn't He just go on in?*

But then I realized that the door had no doorknob. *Ah,* my young mind decided, *Jesus must be a
gentleman who only enters a home where He's welcomed.
Someone has to let Him in. The door has to be opened
from the inside.*

Later I understood that this is the truth of the
gospel. The Master Carpenter didn't forget to put a
doorknob on the outside of our hearts. He simply
chose to only enter a heart that opens from the inside
and welcomes His presence within.

He is still knocking. Can you hear Him?

"Here I am!" He says. "I stand at the door and knock."

2

Masterpiece by the Bay

We are God's workmanship.
EPHESIANS 2:10

*N*orthern California is a gallery of some of God's most magnificent creations. From the majestic redwood-canopied forests to the stately cliffs of the shoreline to the lush vineyards of the Napa Valley wine country, God's handiwork is displayed with splendor. However, I saw one of God's most incredible masterpieces on Alcatraz Island in the middle of San Francisco Bay. He sat at the end of a dark, dank hallway in an abandoned federal prison signing his autobiography *Alcatraz from the Inside*. The white-haired, 80-year-old grandfather with crystal-blue, laughing eyes wore a radiant smile across his wrinkled face. He was Jim Quillen, ex-prisoner #AZ586, and he had spent ten years in this prison built to house the most dangerous criminals of his day. And yet, when I looked into his eyes, he didn't look like a dangerous man.

I didn't have to turn many pages in his book to

discover why. He wrote, "It was only through the grace of our Lord Jesus Christ and His intercession that my life of hopeless incarceration was averted. His help and forgiveness permitted me to obtain freedom, family and a useful productive place in society."

On my trip to San Francisco, I was reminded of God's unchanging strength in the majestic rock cliffs of the shoreline and of His nurturing care as the Vinedresser in the hills of wine country. I saw a picture of God's protective canopy over His children in the towering redwoods. But when I looked into Jim Quillen's eyes, I saw God's most incredible masterpiece...a changed life.

3

The Winner

*I have fought the good fight, I have finished
the race, I have kept the faith.*

2 TIMOTHY 4:7

It was the first swim meet of the year for the newly formed, middle-school aquatic team. The atmosphere was electric with anticipation as 48 adolescents thought of nothing but victory. Justin was among the bunch, and he was swimming the 500-yard freestyle for the first time.

Toward the end of his race everyone had finished…except for Justin. His hands slapped against the water, and it looked like he might go under at any moment. But something kept pushing him onward even though the race had been won eight minutes before.

One teammate, inspired by his brave friend, went to the side of the pool and walked the lane as Justin pressed on.

"Come on, Justin, you can do it! Keep going! Don't give up!"

He was joined by another, then another, until the entire team was walking the length of the pool, encouraging their friend to finish the race. Soon the opposing team saw what was happening and joined in the chant. Previously concerned parents rose to their feet cheering, shouting, and praying. The room pulsated with energy and excitement as teammates and opponents alike pumped courage into one small swimmer.

Twelve long minutes after the starting whistle had blown, an exhausted but smiling Justin swam his final lap and struggled to pull himself out of the pool. The crowd had applauded the swimmer who finished in first place, but they gave Justin a greater cheer for simply finishing the race.

4

The Key to Freedom

It is for freedom that Christ has set us free.
Stand firm, then, and do not let yourselves
be burdened again by a yoke of slavery.
GALATIANS 5:1

North Carolina has birthed some influential men and women. Perhaps one of our favorites is Andy Griffith of the *Andy Griffith Show.* In the fictional town of Mayberry where "Sheriff Andy Taylor" patrolled, there lived a town drunk named Otis. When Otis was arrested for public drunkenness, Andy put him in a jail cell until he sobered up. After a good night's sleep, Otis would stick his hand through the bars of the jail cell door, take the key hanging from a nail on the wall, and let himself out. It was just that simple. On a few occasions Otis stumbled into the jailhouse, grabbed the key, locked himself in the cell, and placed the key back on the nail.

This was always a comical scene, but it reminds me of the jail we can lock ourselves into when we remain prisoners of our pasts. God has set us free, but sometimes we lock ourselves up in the prison of shame and guilt. Our key to freedom isn't hanging by a nail on a jailhouse wall, but He hung by nails on a rugged cross. His name is Jesus. He came to set the prisoner free...for good. And this key is always within our reach. We never have to be locked up again!

Lassie, Come Home!

As the heavens are higher than the earth,
so are my ways higher than your ways
and my thoughts than your thoughts.

ISAIAH 55:9

As a child, my best friend was my collie, Lassie. She was my constant companion, committed confidant, and persistent protector. When the veterinarian told us that Lassie had an incurable skin disease, I was devastated. My dad couldn't bring himself to have her put to sleep, so he took her to an old farmer for the remainder of her days. But it wasn't too long before Lassie ran away.

My dad always looked for Lassie when he was in that neck of the woods. Then one day a miracle happened! Dad saw Lassie running down the road toward him. She looked healthier than ever, and a flurry of fur, tail wagging, and sloppy dog kisses almost knocked Dad off his feet. We were overjoyed when Lassie came cruising home in the gray Buick.

Two weeks later my older brother was outside

wrestling with Lassie in the yard. Before long, he stumbled through the back door ashen faced.

"Mom, we've got a problem," he announced. "Lassie isn't a lassie at all. She's a laddie! She's a boy, and this is not our dog."

Upon closer inspection we discovered that she was indeed a he and not our Lassie after all. We ran ads in the paper, but no one ever claimed him. He seemed perfectly content in our home, so there he stayed.

Have you ever wanted something so badly— hunted, searched, and maybe even prayed—and then, when you found it, you realized it wasn't *exactly* what you wanted, but it was *definitely* what you needed?

I wanted my dog back. Laddie wanted a home. And for one little girl and one stray pup, God's answer was perfect in every way.

Follow Me

*"Follow me," Jesus said to him, and Levi got
up, left everything and followed him.*

Luke 5:27-28

John worked in the family business, and though he was 17, he was reluctant to get his driver's license. Uncle Bob felt the boy was putting off growing up, so he came over one day, took John by the arm, and said, "Boy, it's time to go and get your driver's license."

"But Uncle Bob," John replied, "I haven't practiced enough. I'm not good enough yet."

"Don't you worry about that, son," Bob said. "I'll teach you what you need to know on the way."

The two men, one young with clammy hands and the other older with a knowing grin, drove over to the Department of Motor Vehicles. John parked smack dab in the middle of two spaces with the line running under the middle of the car. He nervously walked into the building, fumbled through the driving test, and miraculously came out with a valid driver's license.

"I wondered how in the world I passed that test," the now older John mused. "Years later I found out. Uncle Bob knew the patrolman who administered it."

And that, my friend, is the gospel. Jesus takes us by the hand. "Follow me," He says. Sometimes we tell Him, "I'm not ready. I need more practice. I'm not good enough yet."

But Jesus says, "Don't you worry about that. You just come with Me, and I'll teach you what you need to know along the way."

And He makes sure we pass the exam...because He knows the One administering the test.

The Redemption Center

*Christ redeemed us from the curse of the
law by becoming a curse for us.*
GALATIANS 3:13

*L*ick. Stick. Lick. Stick.

It was Saturday afternoon, the day Mom and I pasted the S&H Green Stamps in the greenback books. My mom shopped at White's Grocery Store, not because they had the best prices but because they gave S&H Green Stamps with every purchase. For months Mom stuffed stamps in a brown paper bag. Then twice a year we'd pull the bag down from the shelf and stick all the stamps in little booklets. Large stamps represented dollars spent, and only 3 filled a page. Small stamps represented cents spent, and 30 filled a page. I liked doing the dollars.

After hours of pasting the stamps in the books, we enthusiastically drove down to the S&H Redemption Center to trade in our stamps.

"Whatcha goin' to get?" I'd ask as we strolled down the aisle of housewares.

"I don't know," Mom would say. "But it'll be something good!"

After much consideration, Mom would redeem her stamps for a treasure, such as a set of mixing bowls, a new iron, or an electric can opener. Oh yes, it was an exciting day when we went to the S&H Green Stamp Redemption Center!

Looking back on those days, I see a simple picture of the word *redemption*—trading something in for something else, for something valuable.

That's what Jesus did for us when He died on the cross. He traded in His life for ours. He redeemed us. And it all took place at God's redemption center—Calvary's Cross.

It's an exciting day when we visit God's redemption center! Treasures await us at every turn.

The Spelling Train

For when I am weak, then I am strong.

2 CORINTHIANS 12:10

My hands were clammy. Sweat formed on my brow. A familiar knot in the pit of my stomach threatened to push me toward the restroom, and my tongue stuck to the roof of my mouth. It was 10:25 A.M. Just five more minutes and the dreaded event would begin. The first-grade spelling train.

Twenty first graders slipped their munchkin-sized chairs from their desks to form a semicircle around our chief engineer. I always put mine at the end. If we missed the spelling word the teacher held up on a flash card, we had to move to the back of the train. The class chugged along at a quick pace. "Dog. Sally. Bob. Spot. Red. Blue. Mother."

Then it was my turn.

"Sharon, what is this word?"

Pause. Giggles.

More often than not I had no idea. Even if I did know the word, I'd sit in silence, afraid that I would guess incorrectly. I spent most of my time in the first grade in the caboose. As the year progressed, I did move up into the passenger cars a few times, but usually I didn't stay there long enough to keep the seat warm.

That was more than 40 years ago, and now one of my greatest joys is stringing written words together.

I've noticed that life has many unusual twists and turns when God is at the helm. He takes our greatest weaknesses and turns them into our grandest strengths. That's what happens when we turn our lives over to Him—we exit the caboose and get to ride up front with the Engineer to places we never imagined possible.

The Battlefield

Our struggle is not against flesh and blood, but against the rulers, against the authorities, against the powers of this dark world and against the spiritual forces of evil in the heavenly realms.

EPHESIANS 6:12

In my early years I was a rough and rowdy tomboy who climbed trees, skipped rocks, and made skid marks on the asphalt with my pink banana bike. My backyard was the envy of every kid in the neighborhood. It came equipped with a drainage ditch that ran across six city blocks and culminated in a large ditch we dubbed "the canyon."

One afternoon our drainage ditch served as the barrier over which a great battle occurred between our neighborhood boys (myself included) and an opposing neighborhood down the street. Dirt clods were the weapon of choice. However, the rumble was cut short when someone threw a brick that connected with the top of my forehead. Blood poured down my ten-year-old face as I screamed, "You cheated!"

The enemy scattered like flies, and I was rushed to the hospital for stitches. I wore a patch on my forehead like a badge of courage for several days, and my hair never grew back in that spot. But I learned some great life lessons from that dirt clod fight:

1. The enemy cheats.
2. The enemy slings more than just dirt.
3. The enemy has great aim.
4. The enemy's attacks sometime leave scars.
5. The enemy is not playing a game.

I don't fight with bullies anymore—at least not the human kind. But I do have one nemesis who challenges me regularly. The Bible calls him the "great deceiver," "the accuser," "the devil," "the evil one." Interestingly, the same lessons I learned from the dirt clod fight apply to him today.

Grandma's Inheritance

*[Older women] can train the younger women...to
be self-controlled and pure, to be busy at home.*

TITUS 2:4-5

As far back as I can remember, my Grandma Edwards was always old. Her long, gray braid wound around her head like a crown, and her teeth came out at night. A pinch of snuff tucked in her cheek gave her the pick-me-up she needed to get through the day. Grandma never drove a car but rang up the grocery store and a box of supplies would magically appear on her back stoop. The most exciting part of her day was watching *Perry Mason* on her black-and-white television. We drank Coca-Cola from chilled glass bottles and ate peanut butter and crackers while we waited for the verdict to come in.

When I was young I always spent a week with Grandma Edwards. There were no trips to fast-food restaurants or shopping sprees at the mall. I just did what Grandma did: canned beans, made biscuits, shelled peas, and learned to sew. When I was six, we turned a square piece of fabric into a gathered apron. At seven, we transformed a rectangular piece of floral cloth into a jumper. And at eight, we conquered the zipper.

Grandma didn't leave me a sum of money when she passed away, but she left something much more valuable. God used her to turn ordinary days into extraordinary memories. Through her, God showed me that leaving an inheritance to our children is so much more than money in the bank, well-invested mutual funds, and valuable heirlooms. It is leaving them memories of simple times together, instructing them on how to become men and women of God, and leaving a legacy that causes them to "rise up and call you blessed."

Nightmare on York Street

[The devil] is a liar and the father of lies.
JOHN 8:44

Wide-eyed and paralyzed by fear, I pulled the covers up close to my chin and willed myself to fall asleep. The silence was broken only by the pounding of my heart. Dad and I had just watched a scary movie on TV, and I just knew the killers were going to show up at my house any minute.

Sure enough, when my mom went into their bedroom, someone let out a bloodcurdling scream. Something hit the wall with a thud, and Mom began to scream.

The killers were here! I bolted out of bed, jumped out the window, and ran next door for help. Lights sprang to life as I banged on a neighbor's door.

"Someone killed my father, and now they're killing my mom!" I cried.

A phone call home revealed the truth. Dad had been having a bad dream. Just as Mom came into the room and pulled back the covers, the man in Dad's dream was going for the knife, so my dad yelled, which startled my mom, who jumped and hit the wall. It was just a dream. Everything was okay.

I went back home to find my dad looking through all the closets. The nightmare wasn't real, but it sure did feel that way.

That's how Satan works—through fear (False Evidence Appearing Real). He twists the truth, plunders our thoughts, and tries to make us run. He tries to steal our peace, rob our joy, and stir up fear with his lies.

Do a little FBI (Further Bible Investigation) work on the worries of your life. I bet they have Satan's fingerprints all over them. And when it comes to his future demise, this is one movie where you already know the ending. Satan gets his due. And the list of credits is short; there's only one name: Jesus.

The Wreck that Saved Her Life

*We know that in all things God works for
the good of those who love him, who have
been called according to his purpose.*

ROMANS 8:28

For five years Gayle had cortisone injections in her painful knee. Because her mother had joint pain in her knees for most of her adult life, Gayle resigned herself to the same fate—arthritis.

One night Gayle and her husband were out with another couple. She twisted around in the front seat of their car to talk to the couple in the back. As they chatted, she noticed a semitrailer's headlights rapidly approaching their car. Before she could shout a warning, the truck plowed into the back of their car at 55 miles per hour. The driver of the truck had fallen asleep at the wheel and didn't even apply the brakes.

Gayle's car was totaled, but no one in the car was

hurt except Gayle and her arthritic knee, which had been smashed into the dashboard. When she went to the hospital, the doctor X-rayed her injury.

"I don't know how to tell you this," he said when the X-ray results came back, "but you have a slow-growing tumor in your right knee."

"A tumor?" Gayle said. "How long has it been there?"

"Probably for several years. The pain you've had hasn't been arthritis after all. It's been this tumor. If it hadn't been for this accident, we may have never known the truth."

Gayle was scheduled for surgery, and the tumor was removed.

When something seemingly bad happens in our lives, we need to remember that God is the director of the drama of life. We may not understand the "whys" or the "what fors," but we can trust the extraordinary God who controls it all.

Bride in the Box

God...richly provides us with
everything for our enjoyment.
1 TIMOTHY 6:17

There she lay in her beautiful box—a two-foot doll dressed in a white chiffon, pearl-studded wedding gown with matching veil. Her short-cropped, curly brown hair fell softly around her delicate face; her pink, plump skin felt amazingly soft; and her movable eyelids lined with thick black lashes opened and closed with her changing positions. The bride had perfectly shaped lips and crystal-blue eyes that appeared strangely real. She was truly the most beautiful doll I had ever received in my six-year-old life.

My uncle knew of my infatuation with being a bride and had given me this lovely gift. But there was one problem. My mother wouldn't let me play with her.

"You'll have to wait until you're older," she said. "She was very expensive. We'll just keep her in the box until you're big enough to take care of her."

So the doll stayed in her box, safely stowed away in a dresser drawer. Occasionally I'd open the drawer to stroke her hair or straighten up her gown, but never did I take her out and play with her. Now that I'm an adult, I don't even know what became of her.

Thinking back on the lovely gift that was never enjoyed, I'm reminded of the gifts God has given each of us. If we keep those gifts hidden away until we think we're old enough to take proper care of them or mature enough to master them, we'll miss many years of the enjoyment He intended for us. Yes, the gifts may get tattered and torn, but enjoying them will bring the Giver great pleasure. Our enjoyment is His delight. That's what gifts are for.

Are We Having Fun Yet?

Oh, how I love your law!
I meditate on it all day long.
PSALM 119:97

I was 17 years old when about 25 of my jean-clad friends and I sat crossed-legged on the floor of our Christian coffeehouse called "The Ancient of Days." Bell-bottom, hip-hugger pants, tie-dyed T-shirts, long straight hair (on boys and girls), platform shoes...we were a sight. We gathered each week for a Bible study led by a twentysomething fellow from the local college. After singing "Pass It On," the leader grew very serious, lowered his voice, and asked: "Who came here tonight to have...fun?"

My hand was the first to shoot up in the air. As a matter-of-fact, it was the *only* hand raised. I sheepishly looked around the room and mumbled, "Wrong answer?" I felt as though I had a neon sign over my head blinking *Heathen! Heathen!*

With a tsk-tsk look on his face, the young man, just a few years my senior, announced, "We are *not* here to have fun. We are here to study God's Word."

What that whippersnapper didn't understand was that, for me, studying God's Word *is* fun! What could be more exciting than discovering answers to the mysteries of creation, seeing Jesus revealed in the Old Testament, uncovering the truths that can set us free? The Bible is a love story, a murder mystery, a history lesson, a letter from God, and the key to wisdom all wrapped into one.

Wow! The Bible is filled with treasures waiting to be discovered. It was exciting to me when I was 17, and it is still exciting to me today.

So you see, I didn't give the wrong answer after all.

Breaking the Will but Not the Spirit

Submit yourselves, then, to God.
JAMES 4:7

*O*f all of the activities ten-year-old Miriam enjoyed, she loved riding her horse, Charlie, the best. He had a sleek chestnut mane, well-defined legs, and a strong will to match. Miriam felt powerful and self-assured when controlling this massive animal— except when they returned from a jaunt in the woods. As soon as they got close enough for Charlie to catch a glimpse of the barn, he bolted homeward, forcing Miriam to hang on for dear life.

One day Miriam's riding instructor witnessed this strong-willed animal taking control.

"Miriam!" she called out. "You can't let that animal control you in that manner. Bring that horse back out of the barn this instant!"

Dutifully Miriam mounted Charlie and rode him a distance away from the stalls.

"Now, when you turn around and Charlie sees the barn and begins to run toward it," the instructor said, "pull the reins all the way to the right. Do not let him go forward."

On cue Miriam steered her horse toward the stalls. On cue he bolted.

"Turn him! Turn him!" the instructor shouted.

Young Miriam pulled the reins to the right as hard as she could until the horse's head was inches from his right shoulder. Charlie fought her with the force of a war horse. Round and round the horse and rider circled.

After ten long minutes, Charlie stopped circling. Miriam gently tapped his flanks, and he slowly walked toward the stable. She had broken his will, and he now obeyed his master's touch.

It is an extraordinary moment with God when we stop going in circles, yield our will to the Master, and walk at a steady pace wherever He leads.

A Courageous Queen

*For momentary, light affliction is producing for us
an eternal weight of glory far beyond all comparison.*

2 CORINTHIANS 4:17 (NASB)

Katie was only 11 years old when the doctors removed her cancerous leg below the knee. She felt her young life was over.

"Who will ever want me?" she cried. "I'll never be able to walk or run again."

Katie did learn how to walk, and life returned to a new kind of normal, though she kept her prosthesis hidden from the world. But then God began nudging Katie to return to the hospital where she had her surgery to talk to other children facing similar ordeals. She put her fears aside and visited the cancer ward and showed a girl named Amanda her leg.

"Here, go ahead and touch it," she said. "It's okay." And Katie saw something flicker in Amanda's eyes. It was hope.

Katie graduated from high school and attended the University of Central Arkansas. While there she saw a TV program about a double amputee who had become an athlete and a model. This amputee even showed various prostheses she used for different occasions.

So Katie decided it was time to stop hiding her leg from the world, and she did it in a big way. She entered the Miss University of Central Arkansas pageant! She participated in the talent, evening gown, and interview competitions. But she won the hearts of the crowd when she proudly walked down the catwalk during the bathing suit competition. There have been many tearful moments as pageant sponsors have placed the crown on a winner's head. But I daresay there was never a more precious moment than when Katie Signaigo was crowned Miss UCA.

No, Katie's life was not over when the doctors removed her leg to save her. It was the beginning of an exciting journey filled with many extraordinary moments with God.

The Unsecured Window

*Be self-controlled and alert. Your enemy
the devil prowls around like a roaring
lion looking for someone to devour.*

1 PETER 5:8

A mysterious tapping came from the bathroom window as I put on the finishing touches of my makeup one September night. I turned off the overhead light to get a better view. When I did, I saw the outline of a man peering in at me through the second-story window. My heart pounded as my feet stood frozen in place. Then, as if propelled by the invisible hand of God, I ran down the stairs and out the front door. I fled to a neighbor's house and rushed into her kitchen.

"Sharon, what's wrong?" Mrs. Scarborough asked.

I stood silenced by fear.

"Sharon, look at me," Mrs. Scarborough said again. "What's wrong?"

"There's a man looking in my window," I finally managed to say.

Mrs. Scarborough called the police, and within minutes uniformed men were scouring the premises for clues.

After I calmed down, I realized the real danger. This part of our home was a later addition, and the upstairs bathroom window was the only window in the entire house that didn't have a lock. I suspect the potential intruder knew that.

The Bible tells us of another enemy that roams around like a roaring lion seeking someone to devour. And like the perpetrator, he is always looking for the unsecured window or the unlocked door—an area of our lives that we've left unprotected. We must purpose to guard our hearts, for an unsecured window of the soul is an invitation for the enemy to creep in and wreak havoc on our lives. And he wants to do more than look. He'll take advantage of any access he can find.

I Want, I Need, God Wants Me to Have

Godliness with contentment is great gain.
1 TIMOTHY 6:6

Mary Elizabeth was strolling down the cookie aisle at Wal-Mart with her three-year-old daughter, Sarah, riding comfortably in the front seat of the shopping buggy. Suddenly Sarah spied a box of sugar cookies coated with pink icing and decorated with multicolored sprinkles.

Her eyes brightened as she put on her best cherub face. "Mommy, I *want* those cookies."

"Oh, Sarah," her mom said, "we don't need any cookies today. We have plenty at home. Maybe another time."

Ten minutes later, as Mary Elizabeth passed through the checkout line, Sarah tried again.

"Mommy, I *need* those cookies."

"No, Sarah, you don't need those cookies. We have plenty at home, and I'm not buying cookies today."

Finally, as they pulled out of the Wal-Mart parking lot, Sarah gave it one last try.

"Mommy, I think *God wants me to have* those cookies."

I laughed as my friend told me this story. It was a nervous laugh. For just a moment I saw myself riding through life in a shopping buggy, pointing at first one thing and then another, whining, "I want…I need…I think God wants me to have."

Sarah already had learned how we justify our whims. Whether it's sugar cookies with sprinkles on top or a new red convertible, given enough time, we can justify most of our wants. For Sarah, she went from *I want* to *I need* to *God wants me to have* in a matter of minutes. For us it may take a little longer, but the tendency is still there.

God says He will supply us with everything we *need,* and that is often a far cry from everything we *want.*

Grandma's Hands

[She] extends her hands to the needy.
PROVERBS 31:20

On a shelf in my living room sits a black-and-white photograph of my Grandmother Anderson. I'm always drawn to her hands that seem much too large for her petite frame, and I'm reminded of all the places a mother's hands go during her child's life.

Our hands grip the bedrail in pain in the delivery room, and then gently caress our newborns for the first time. Before long those hands are changing diapers, washing bottoms and faces, cleaning spit-up, wiping tears, rocking sleepyheads, and placing babies in their cribs. Then they are holding toddlers' chubby hands or grabbing them to keep them out of harm's way. Tossing a ball, preparing holiday dinners, setting a festive table, tying packages for birthday parties and Christmas celebrations. Coloring and cutting out shapes in workbooks. Picking up leaves and bugs for collections. Pushing swings and letting go of bikes as children first learn to pedal on their own. Sewing party dresses and mending torn baseball jerseys, washing scraped knees and spooning out medicine. Holding the sweaty palms of awkward adolescents while dancing around the den. Tying neckties and pinning on boutonnieres for a first party. Writing letters to children away at camp and folding hands in prayer asking for God's protection. Tightly grasping the steering wheel while chauffeuring children from one place to the next or gripping the seat as teens learn how to drive. Hands that wave goodbye as a son drives off to college and hands that adjust a cherished daughter's wedding veil.

Children are gifts from God, and with our hands and our hearts we release them to Him.

The Hidden Key

The thief comes only to steal and kill and destroy.
JOHN 10:10

I grew up in a sleepy little town in eastern North Carolina that had a railroad track running down the middle of downtown that divided it into two counties. We slept with our windows open, our doors unlocked, and rode our bicycles all over town without reservation.

But things changed in the early seventies. We began to keep our windows closed at night, our doors locked even during the day, and kids stayed much closer to home. At our house we kept an extra key in the mailbox just inside the garage. The only people who knew it was there were our family members and the mailman…or so we thought.

In high school, when I went home for lunch every day, I simply reached into the mailbox to retrieve the key, and then placed it back in the box until I came home again in the afternoon.

One day I came home after school at the usual

time, used the hidden key, and let myself in. I made a beeline to the television to turn on my favorite program, but when I opened the cabinet, I discovered the TV was missing. We'd been robbed! The thief had apparently used the hidden key!

That's what Satan does in our lives. He watches us and knows exactly where that hidden key to our secret places lies. Then, at the most opportune time, he unlocks the door to steal our peace and joy. There's only one solution to his thievery: Don't hide the key. Give God the key to your heart—your whole heart—and never worry about being robbed again.

Adopted

In love he predestined us to be adopted
as his sons through Jesus Christ, in
accordance with his pleasure and will.

EPHESIANS 1:5

Debbie took her 13-year-old son, Jason, to the dermatologist to have a few suspicious moles checked out. The doctor asked her, "Has anyone on your or your husband's side of the family had melanoma or any other type of skin cancer?"

"No, I can't think of any," she replied.

The doctor asked a few other questions about their family history and then wrapped up the exam.

When he left the room, Jason looked up at Debbie and said, "Mom, when the doctor asked about your family history, it doesn't matter. I'm adopted!"

"You're right, Jason," she said. "I totally forgot."

Debbie had gone through five years of infertility treatments and two years of waiting to adopt a child. Eight months after she adopted Jason, she found out she was pregnant with Jordan. Amazingly, these boys have looked like twins for much of their lives. It's only as the boys have grown into young men that I can even tell them apart.

It was an extraordinary moment for Jason when he realized that his mom had forgotten he was adopted. He was simply her son. Ephesians 1:5 says that we have been adopted as sons [and daughters] through Jesus Christ. God has chosen us to be His own, adopted into His family.

I think that God, like Debbie, probably forgets we're adopted. He just sees us as His children.

22

Put a Lid on It

> The tongue is a small part of the body, but it
> makes great boasts. Consider what a great
> forest is set on fire by a small spark.
>
> JAMES 3:5

My dad woke from his nap to the sounds of his daughter's screams as I stood in the middle of a kitchen engulfed in flames. I'd been making candles for weeks. Our kitchen looked like a prosthesis laboratory with candles in the shape of praying hands littering the counters. In the middle of a waxing and wicking session, I walked away to answer the doorbell and forgot about the molten wax simmering on the stove. My friend and I walked back into the kitchen to discover flames pouring from the pot. In a panic he threw a glass of water on the fire, and the flames exploded. Fire crawled up the wall, across the ceiling, and down the other side of the room.

Dad awoke with a start and saw me surrounded by flames, and with the agility of a superhero he ran into the kitchen. Faster than a speeding bullet, he grabbed the lid of the pot and clamped it down on the source of the flames. As quickly as the fire had erupted, it receded...like a genie returning to his bottle.

I was amazed at how fast the flames engulfed the room. I thought of the feeling of the fire licking my hair and the terrifying sound of the blaze. It made me think about my words and how easily they can explode and singe those around me.

The Bible says that our words are like sparks that can ignite an entire forest fire. Suddenly I understood how quickly that can happen.

But my dad showed me how to stop the fire from spreading. It's simple really. Just put a lid on it.

The Interview

*Believe in the Lord Jesus, and you will
be saved—you and your household.*

ACTS 16:31

My palms were clammy as I waited in the small
room for my first job interview. Dr. Ford,
the man who would decide my professional destiny,
was somewhat intimidating, but I was ready for
whatever he had to throw at me.

Let the games begin, I mused.

And so they did.

"What was the last book you read?" he asked.
"What did you eat for breakfast?" "What is your least
favorite household job?"

I answered each question honestly, but I wondered, *What does this have to do with being a dental
hygienist? Is this what I've studied so hard for?*

After 45 minutes of rapid-fire questioning and
chitchat, Dr. Ford leaned forward and said, "Sharon,
we'd like you to join our team."

I looked him in the eye and asked, "Aren't you

even going to ask me what kind of grades I made in school?"

Mortified, I could not believe those words escaped my practiced lips.

Dr. Ford threw back his head and filled the room with thunderous laughter. "I imagine they were pretty good," he said with a twinkle in his eye.

Later I understood that Dr. Ford was more interested in my character than my credentials, and what was in my heart than in my head.

I imagine when we have our very last interview, that moment when we approach the gates of heaven, God won't ask how well we've performed on earth. He won't care about our trophies or ribbons of achievement. Like my first interview so long ago, God won't be as concerned with what's in our heads but what's in our hearts.

And that's one interview I'm looking forward to.

24

Refinished and Restored

If anyone is in Christ, he is a new creation;
the old has gone, the new has come!

2 CORINTHIANS 5:17

S haron, do you realize how much time and
energy it's going to take to refinish that old
table and chairs?" my mother asked as she perused
my latest purchase.

When I was a teenager I had a fetish for antiques
and old furniture and bought a number of pieces at
auctions, flea markets, and estate sales. Often when
I brought my treasures home, my family would roll
their eyes and say, "I can't believe you paid money
for that dirty piece of junk."

But I never saw my purchases as junk. They just
needed a little work...okay, a lot of work. Thinking
back, I believe my love for refinishing old beat-up
furniture had something to do with how I viewed
my life and how God refinished me.

Like the old table, I was on the auctioning
block, and God purchased me with Christ's blood.

I had layers and layers of my old self that had to be stripped away to reveal the beauty hidden beneath. God sanded me with life experiences and trials to remove my rough edges. He glued my loose joints and mended my broken pieces. Then He put a sealer on me and in me—the Holy Spirit—who brought out the beauty of who God created me to be.

After I finished refurbishing the old table and chairs, I sat in the garage thinking about all God had done in my life. My mom opened the door, looked at the old table, and said, "Oh my. I never thought something so ugly could turn out so beautiful."

I said, "Amen."

25

No Clams for Larry

Give thanks to the LORD, for he is good;
his love endures forever.

1 CHRONICLES 16:34

"I'm not going to pray in a public place!" Larry announced.

A group of my friends gathered at the Sanitary Fish Market for platters of fried shrimp, fish, and clams. It was a strange name for a restaurant, but the food was great. Even at 18 I always bowed my head and said a simple prayer before eating...all of us did except Larry. Larry was a macho man who claimed to be in control of his own destiny. He didn't need God. So when we bowed our heads to pray, Larry held his head high.

We all ordered clam chowder as an appetizer. We had the same waitress and the same chowder from the same pot. We three "holy rollers," as Larry called us, dipped our spoons into our bowls and tasted chowder full of tender clams and steamy potatoes. Then proud Larry dipped in his spoon and retrieved only broth.

"Why is your bowl so full of clams?" he complained. "All I've got is broth."

"Well, maybe it's because we asked God to bless ours and you didn't," I said.

Larry didn't complain to the fine people at the Sanitary; he ate "crow" instead.

Sometimes we like what life serves up and sometimes we don't. But most of the time it simply depends on the attitude and the gratitude of the person holding the spoon.

26

Buddy Breathing

*If one falls down,
his friend can help him up.*

ECCLESIASTES 4:10

*L*et's go scuba diving!" a friend exclaimed one hot summer day.

"That sounds great," I said. "But I don't know how."

"Just leave it to me," he said.

I was 17 the first time I went scuba diving. My friend strapped an oxygen tank on his back, a mask on his face, and flippers on his feet. I only had a mask and flippers.

"Where's my oxygen?" I asked.

"I've got it," he answered as he patted the tank on his back.

So into the ocean we plunged. He put his arm around my waist as if I were a sack of potatoes and down we went. John drew oxygen from the tank and then passed the breathing apparatus to me. We took turns breathing the oxygen in what he called "buddy breathing." It occurred to me that I was totally dependent on this young boy to keep me alive!

Throughout my life the words of friends have been like oxygen when I felt as if I were drowning. God has sent people my way who have strapped on the Word of God and passed the life-giving words to me when I've needed them most.

Buddy breathing. That's what we can do for each other when a friend forgets how to draw in the air she needs. That's what God does for us each time we open His Word.

27

Butterflies

*We, who with unveiled faces all reflect the
Lord's glory, are being transformed into his
likeness with ever-increasing glory, which
comes from the Lord, who is the Spirit.*

2 CORINTHIANS 3:18

She flits and flutters her wings like a flirting young damsel batting feathery eyelashes at a suitor. Her yellow wings are jeweled with black and hints of red, and delicate tiny feet dance on pink and purple bouquets. A gust of wind lifts her, and she seems to float in search of something unseen. Returning to her mission, she skims the surface of several blossoms until she alights on one that pleases her. She perches daintily on a violet petunia and sips as if having her afternoon tea.

I love to watch butterflies drink from the flowers in my backyard. It never ceases to amaze me that these beautiful creatures are birthed from such an ugly brown wrapping. They remind me of my own emergence as a creature of freedom and flight.

Like a butterfly I was held captive in a deep, dark chrysalis of fear. But the time was not for naught. God was shaping and molding me into a beautiful, colorful creation. Like the caterpillar undergoing a momentous change in the confining chrysalis, I had to go through a sometimes difficult healing process to be free of hurts from the past. The caterpillar takes days to be transformed, but emerges strong enough to fly. I had to fight for years, but God used the trials to change me, to give me the strength to take flight and soar.

It was an extraordinary moment with God that taught me the necessity of the "chrysalis years" to develop strength and character to fly. And what a joy to soar to heights unimaginable via the breath of the Savior who makes all things beautiful in His time.

28

From Death to Life

*But because of his great love for us, God, who
is rich in mercy, made us alive with Christ
even when we were dead in transgressions.*

EPHESIANS 2:4

Julianna came out of the womb ready to meet every challenge with determination, every celebration with enthusiasm, and every mystery with the passion of discovery. The fiery redhead lived life with the throttle wide open.

At 12 years old, Julianna graced the dance floor with other aspiring ballerinas. One unforgettable Thursday, a neighbor came to pick her up for dance class. In usual fashion Julianna rushed out like a whirlwind and slammed the door behind her. However, the door closed before all of her made it across the threshold. Julianna spun around, threw the door open, and made a horrible discovery.

"Help!" she screamed. "I just cut my finger off!"

Sure enough, Julianna had amputated the upper third of the middle finger on her right hand. She was rushed to the hospital where they put Humpty Dumpty back together again.

Several days later Julianna and her mother removed the bandage to reveal a dead, mushroom-like thimble on top of her finger.

"Don't worry," the doctor assured them. "Underneath the dead part that I grafted back on, a new finger, complete with nerves and blood vessels is forming."

Four weeks after the incident I received a letter from my little redheaded friend. At the bottom she wrote, "P.S. My crusty thimble fell off, and I have a new finger!"

Now don't ask me how this transformation happened. It's a mystery to me. But Scripture tells us of another grafting procedure that is even more astounding. Though we were spiritually dead—cut off and rotten to the core—God demonstrated His love for us by grafting us onto the living root, Jesus Christ, and making us alive together with Him.

Now that's a real miracle!

29

The Gift

The greatest of these is love.
1 CORINTHIANS 13:13

*Y*ou'll need that."

"That'll come in handy."

"You can never have too many mixing bowls."

These comments were interspersed with numerous oohs and aahs during my first bridal shower. I sat among mounds of various sized boxes wrapped in shiny silver and glossy-white paper topped with beautifully crafted bows. Openings revealed toaster ovens, electric can openers, stainless steel mixing bowls, and fine china. But the grand finale was a large box from my mom.

My mother was one of 12 children raised on a farm in eastern North Carolina. During her fifth year of marriage she discovered she was pregnant. To pass the time, she learned to crochet using household twine—the same twine used on their tobacco farm to tie up the amber leaves to dry. She didn't know a lot about the fine gauge of 100-percent wool skeins of yarn, but she knew about the strength and durability of 100-percent cotton twine.

During the nine months she carried me in her womb, Mom's nimble fingers crafted a beautifully crocheted bedspread. Love was woven into every stitch. The last of the fringe was tatted in place a few days before I made my grand debut. She tucked the bedspread away for this very day, 23 years later.

Everyone crowded around to watch as I opened Mom's gift. I carefully plucked the bow from its lid, tore away the elegant wrapping, and removed the top. Gently I folded back layers of tissue paper to reveal the beautiful masterpiece Mom created while God created me.

"You can never have too many bedspreads," one of the old-timers said.

"And you can never have too much love," I replied.

30

God's Speedometer

Do not conform any longer to the pattern of this world,
but be transformed by the renewing of your mind.

ROMANS 12:2

My husband's first car was a 12-year-old Volkswagen Beetle with several remarkable features: no air conditioner, no defroster, and no seat belts. The speedometer had stopped when the odometer reached 200,000 miles and never ticked again.

"How do you know how fast you're going?" I asked him on our first date.

"Easy," he said. "I pace myself by how fast everyone else is going."

So Steve traveled around town, on highways and byways, with no earthly idea how fast he was driving.

Ten months after our first date, Steve and I were married. He drove 200 miles for our wedding, leaving in the wee hours of the morning to avoid the midday heat on that August weekend. Because it was early, there was no traffic...and Steve needed traffic to gauge his speed.

Two hours into the trip he saw a blue light flashing in his rearview mirror. He explained to the officer that he was on his way to get married. The patrolman just smiled as he handed Steve the ticket and said, "Well, don't let this ruin your day."

I was upset with the patrolman, but the reality is that cars are not meant to be driven without speedometers. Then God reminded me, *Neither are you*. We are not to pace ourselves according to those around us—how others live and the decisions they make. We are to look into the Bible for our standard of living and let God set our pace.

We didn't let the ticket ruin our wedding day. It went off without a hitch (except ours, of course). And we enjoyed a wonderful honeymoon...which we took in a borrowed car.

31

Messenger from Heaven

*Never will I leave you;
never will I forsake you.*

HEBREWS 13:5

"Katie, you have pancreatic cancer and three to six months to live," the doctor said.

Three months! Katie replayed her past 50 years and her mind filled with frantic questions: *How did this happen? What went wrong? How did I get to this point?*

Katie had accepted Jesus as her Savior when she was a little girl, but she'd strayed far from the godly path. Like the woman at the well, Katie thought about her two failed marriages, and the man she was living with who was not her husband.

"Lord, you know all I've done," Katie prayed. "Is this why I'm sick? Am I being punished? People have told me that You still love me, but I feel so alone."

Katie reached for her Bible. It fell open to Luke 3:22, and she read about the Holy Spirit descending on Jesus like a dove. Tears streamed down her cheeks. "Where are You, Lord? Please don't desert me."

Katie turned to look at the sun glistening over the tranquil lake in her backyard. Suddenly a dove fluttered to her windowsill and perched on its ledge. Katie hugged her Bible to her chest as she and the dove locked eyes. She saw God's answer.

Yes, Katie, I do love you, He seemed to say. *You may have strayed from the path that I marked out for you, but that hasn't changed My love. I never left you, and I'll stay right here by your side until the day I come to take you home.*

Three months later the dove came again to Katie. Only this time when He soared back toward heaven, Katie's spirit went home with Him.

32

Make Each Moment Count

I will sing to the LORD all my life;
I will sing praise to my God as long as I live.

When I was newly married, I attended a social club meeting of women whose husbands shared the same profession. There was nothing wrong with the gathering, but I walked away feeling as though I'd wasted a precious gift—a morning of my life.

The next month I opted not to attend. Instead I went to a nursery to pick out some flowers to plant in my garden. While musing among the impatiens and begonias, I spotted Carol, a woman whose husband was also in the same profession as mine. Two little girls clambered about her as she carefully chose blue, pink, and yellow perennials that would bloom year after year. Carol had cancer and had been given only a few months to live.

Suddenly God whispered in my ear, *Sharon, if you knew you had only a few months to live, would you be at the social club or buying flowers with your children?*

It was a poignant moment as I was reminded of the brevity of life and what is most precious to me—my family and my faith. We never know how much or how little time we have on this earth. I've resolved to spend each day as if it were my last...to make each day count.

Mrs. Jaynes, You're Leading Again

Wives, submit to your husbands as to the Lord.
EPHESIANS 5:22

Mrs. Jaynes, you're leading again," the ballroom dancing instructor said as she tapped me on the shoulder.

Why was it so difficult for me to relinquish control? Why would I not yield to Steve's gentle press or release? Why was I having so much trouble allowing him to lead?

"Your husband has the most difficult role," the instructor said. "He has to learn all the steps, and all you have to do is follow. His job is to make you look good, but you must be responsive to his cues."

Then I had an extraordinary moment with God as He reminded me of the symbiotic dance of marriage. The dance class was a microcosm of what God intended for marriage. Two people moving as one.

Coming together and moving apart—ever connected. Fluid artistry of movement designed by God.

God then expanded on the lesson and showed me that He is the ultimate leader in the dance of life, and sometimes I refuse to relinquish control to Him. I refuse to yield to His gentle nudges and guiding touches. *I can do this on my own,* I boast. But then the dance becomes muddled, and I trip over my own two feet. Then there are no beautiful waltzes through my days or rhythmic cha-chas in time with God's beat of life. I stumble and fall when I take the lead.

But in the dance of days, when God guides me with His gentle hand and I relinquish control to my Leader, our feet move as one through the twists and turns, twirls and tilts. The flow is a choreographed masterpiece of movement, beauty, and grace.

34

Reflexes

Train yourself to be godly.
1 Timothy 4:7

*I*t was hot. The traffic was heavy. I was distracted. I was driving alone, headed home from the North Carolina coast. The July traffic was bumper to bumper with everyone going faster than the posted speed limit. I had other things on my mind when I felt the right front tire of my sporty two-tone Pontiac Sunbird slip off the asphalt and onto the gravel shoulder. I heard the voice of my driver's ed instructor from years before: "If you run off the road, do not, and I repeat, do not jerk your car back on the road. Slow to a stop and gently guide the car back on the road."

My mind knew the rule. I was even repeating "do not jerk the car" when, in a flood of panic, I promptly jerked the car. I pulled the steering wheel to the left, then to the right, and then lost control. The car headed down an embankment and began to roll like a toy tossed by an angry child. The demolished car landed upside down at the bottom of the hill, and miraculously I crawled out the window without a scratch.

It was an extraordinary moment with God when He spared my life, but it was also an extraordinary lesson on the power of reflexes. Sometimes we know in our heads what we are supposed to do, but the reflexes of old programming overcome reason. Only through prayer and practice can we retrain our old ways and habits to form new godly reflexes that will reflect the nature of Christ.

35

Would You Be Afraid?

Why are you so afraid? Do you still have no faith?

MARK 4:40

She was among an eager group of four-year-old children crowded around my feet as I taught their Sunday school lesson about Jesus and His disciples caught in a horrific storm on the Sea of Galilee.

"The winds bleeeeew and rocked the little boat back and forth. The waves were soooo big they splashed over the wooden sides and got the men all wet. The water started filling up the boat. Do you know what happens when a boat gets full of water?"

"It sinks!" they shouted together.

"That's right," I continued with a concerned look on my face. "The lightning was soooooo bright it lit up the night sky, and the thunder was sooooo loud they could feel it vibrate in their chests."

Thinking I would have my audience a little worried about the men in the boat, I asked, "Now if *you* were in a tiny boat, caught in a terrible storm like this, would *you* be afraid?"

Then one precious little girl, confident and unshaken by the entire scenario, shrugged her shoulders and calmly said, "Not if Jesus was in the boat with me."

Suddenly I realized she was the real teacher that day.

Just as the disciples had the storm raging all around them, storms often rage around us. A friend discovers she has cancer, a husband loses a job, a child is born with a defect. Waves of emotions threaten to fill our lives and toss us into the inky ocean of despair.

"Tell me, would you be afraid?"
"Not if Jesus was in the boat with me."

In the midst of the raging storms of life, we need never be afraid. He *is always* in the boat with us—and that brings peace to a troubled soul.

36

An Easter Bride

*For the wedding of the Lamb has come,
and his bride has made herself ready.*

REVELATION 19:7

It was a beautiful day for a wedding. The sun shone brightly as daffodils danced in the gentle breeze, nodding their happy faces in conversation. A choir of robins, cardinals, and finches sang rounds of cheerful melodies that floated through a clear blue sky, and the air had that crisp quality of spring, the chill from winter's past mingled with the warmth of summer's promise. It was Easter Sunday, the day the groom had chosen to come and get His bride.

Iris had been waiting for Him to come and steal her away her entire life. She wore a white dress with flecks of blue and held a bouquet of pink carnations with a spray of asparagus fern as wispy as her baby-fine hair. A sweet smile spread across her 74-year-old face. I closed my eyes and imagined her walking into her beloved Jesus' waiting arms as He held out His hand to help her across the threshold to eternity.

On a beautiful Easter Sunday, my husband's dear Aunt Iris went home to be with her Lord. As we all gathered around to say our last goodbyes, I could not mourn. She hadn't been married in this lifetime, and I envisioned her joining Jesus Christ as His bride... what she had longed for her entire life.

For me it wasn't a funeral; it was a wedding. And she was a beautiful Easter bride.

37

Lame Man Dancing

My lover spoke and said to me,
"Arise, my darling,
my beautiful one, and come with me."
SONG OF SONGS 2:10

teve and I stumbled around the dance floor in a crowded restaurant. Other couples moved as one around the floor as we hid in the back so no one could see our awkward steps. That's when I saw them, the last couple to approach, with no hesitation at all…the wife in a sparkling gown, the husband in a wheelchair.

He was a balding, large-framed man with a neatly trimmed beard. On his left hand he wore a white glove, perhaps to cover a skin disease. As the band played a peppy tune, his wife held his healthy right hand and danced back and forth with her love. He never rose from the wheelchair, but they didn't seem to care. They came together and separated like expert dancers. He spun her around as she stooped to conform to his seated position. Lovingly, like a fairy child, she danced around his chair, and their laughter became the fifth instrument in the four-piece band. And even though his feet never moved from their metal resting places, his shoulders swayed in perfect time and his eyes danced with hers. Their radiant smiles lit up the room with a torch of love.

While other couples had impressed the crowd with perfect steps and graceful movements, this last couple moved the room to tears. God showed me that it is not perfect steps or a perfect life that the world longs to see. It is a genuine display of love that truly moves the heart. *You dance with Me,* He seemed to say, *and our love will amaze the world.*

That night God sent a lame man to teach me how to dance.

38

Full Power

*[I pray] that you may know...his incomparably
great power for us who believe.*

EPHESIANS 1:18-19

I'm moving in!" I announced to the bewildered
builder. Our new house wasn't quite finished, but
I was tired of waiting. It didn't have electrical hookup
yet, but I figured if the construction workers could
operate from the little bit of electricity from a saw box
attached to the power pole, I could too.

"Okay, Mrs. Jaynes," the builder said. "You can
move in, but you can turn on only a few lights at a
time. If you want to take a hot shower, you'll have to
turn everything else off for the water to heat up. You
can turn on the oven, but you can't have anything
else on at the same time. If you move into this house,
it will be like camping out in a very nice tent."

Yes! I had won! We moved in.

It was fun at first, but I quickly grew tired of cold
showers and takeout meals. And candlelight dinners
soon lost their appeal. We were thrilled when the

electrician removed the temporary box and flipped the switch to give us full power. I turned on all the lights, fired up the oven, and took a hot shower...all at the same time.

I thought of how this situation is similar to our Christian walk. Sometimes we live off partial power spiritually. We have access to the power of God through the Holy Spirit. Why do we settle for a few volts when we could operate fully charged with all circuits wide open?

When I mentioned this to God, He reminded me that His power is always available. We just need to connect to the true Power Source every day.

39

Emergency! Emergency!

*Call to me and I will answer you and tell you
great and unsearchable things you do not know.*

JEREMIAH 33:3

he phone rang at 2:00 A.M. I groggily picked up
the receiver and managed a weak "Hello."

"My son is having a terrible toothache," the caller
said. "Is the doctor in?"

(My husband is a dentist, and at nights and on
weekends I serve as his ready, reliable receptionist.)

"Yes, ma'am, the doctor is in. How long has this
tooth been bothering your son?"

"Oh, I'd say for about two weeks," she said.

So why did you wait until now to call? (I didn't
say this out loud, of course.) As I continued gathering information, something seemed odd. So I asked,
"Ma'am, how old is your son?"

"Twenty-seven. My son is 27 years old."

I sat up in bed so quickly, I accidentally jerked
the phone cord out of the wall and disconnected
the caller. She didn't call back. I'd envisioned a

distraught mother with a crying 7-year-old. But 27? Oh my.

I lay back down complaining and grumbling. "Lord, why is it that people won't go to the doctor regularly but want help on demand when they have an emergency?"

When I got quiet enough to listen, I heard God reply, "Now you know how I feel."

40

Don't Let Him In

*Sin is crouching at your door; it desires
to have you, but you must master it.*

GENESIS 4:7

How did this happen? How am I going to get this man out of my house?

Questions raced through my mind as the vacuum cleaner salesman moved from room to room sprinkling his demonstration trash on my floor and then sucking it up with his machine. For over an hour this man informed me about the danger of dust mites and the benefits of his equipment.

"I already have a vacuum cleaner," I said.

"But not like this one, you don't!"

Finally I managed to convince this determined salesman that I wasn't interested in his vacuum cleaner. He was still talking as I shoved him out the door.

Whew! What just happened here? I whispered to God as I leaned against the closed door. *Where did I go wrong?*

You let him in, God said.

Of course. God was right. I should never have let the man enter my house. Then God reminded me that I had just witnessed an example of how to win every spiritual battle. When a tempting thought comes knocking at the door, don't answer it. When a deceptive idea rings the bell, don't let it in. Once a thought crosses the threshold of the mind, it's very difficult to get it to leave. Victory is possible, but it will save much heartache and pain if we don't allow the salesman in to sprinkle his trash in our minds to begin with.

We don't want what he's selling anyway.

41

When We Don't Understand

One thing God has spoken,
two things have I heard:
that you, O God, are strong,
and that you, O Lord, are loving.

PSALM 62:11-12

"Mommy, Mommy!" Steven cried. "Don't let them hurt me!"

Steven was two years old when he contracted a severe case of the flu. He slumped listlessly in my lap like an old rag doll. When I carried my limp little one into the doctor's office, he quickly surmised that Steven was dehydrated and needed to be admitted to the hospital immediately.

My heart broke as the nurses strapped my little boy onto a table and began placing an IV into his tiny arm.

"Mommy, make them stop!" he cried "They're hurting me!"

"No, honey, they're going to make you all better," I said.

Steven cried. I cried. The nurses cried.

I could only imagine what was going through Steven's little mind: *Why are these people hurting me? Why doesn't Mommy make them stop? She must not love me. She's not protecting me. If she loved me she wouldn't let them do this. She must not care about me!*

God was giving me a glimpse into how He feels when I'm going through a painful situation that is for my benefit. "I thought You loved me?" I cry out. "Why have You deserted me? Why don't You make it stop!"

But even when I don't understand, when I can't see His plan, I know that all His ways are loving and kind. He knows what's best for me and allows the painful remedy to do its healing work.

42

A Way of Escape

*God is faithful; he will not let you be tempted
beyond what you can bear. But when you
are tempted, he will also provide a way
out so that you can stand up under it.*

1 CORINTHIANS 10:13

A little fluorescent-green fly with transparent wings positioned itself on the dashboard of my car like a runner waiting on his mark. Then it torpedoed into the windshield at breakneck speed, only to bounce back from the invisible shield. Confused, it perched on the dashboard once again and strategized its next move, while rubbing its tiny little hands together. Suddenly it shot forward with all its might, only to once again bounce off and land on the dash. Then, in one final act of desperation, it attacked the glass with frantic fury.

Feeling rather sorry for this insect, I rolled down my window and spoke softly, "Look, little fly, the window is open. Here's your way of escape."

The fly was oblivious to the freedom just inches

away, so I tried to coax it out. It resisted like a puppy on a leash and perched on the edge of the window with its wings pinned back by the 60-mile-per-hour wind.

"Go on," I coaxed. "What are you waiting for?"

Finally I gave him the push he needed, and he was free.

Why was I so concerned for this silly fly? Pity, I guess. It was trying so hard to get free, and yet the way of escape was right in front of him. That's not so very different from you and me. God always provides a way of escape—a brightly lit exit sign over the door that leads away from temptation. He coaxes us to safety with gentle nudges of freedom, but in the end the choice is ours.

43

The Blanket

I will lie down and sleep in peace,
for you alone, O LORD,
make me dwell in safety.

PSALM 4:8

"Where's my blanket?" towheaded little Steven asked when we returned home from a trip.

"I think we left it at Grandma's house," I answered.

"We'll have to go back and get it," he decided.

"Honey, we can't. Grandma's house is too far away. You'll just have to do without it."

For four years Steven's yellow blanket had been his nighttime companion. It was Steven's security, comfort, and friend. During naptime I'd watch as he clutched his blanket under his arm and rubbed his fingers together over one particular satin-covered corner.

"This is my part," he'd say with a smile.

But there came a time in Steven's little-boy life when it was time to give up the blanket, and I knew I had to leave it at Grandma's.

Steven had a fitful night's sleep as he snuggled in his bed for the first time without the comfort and security of his faithful friend. But as the days and weeks passed, his longing for the blanket subsided. Pretty soon he forgot about it altogether.

Thinking back on Steven's yellow blanket causes me to consider what *I* cling to for security. Do I depend on the approval of friends? A tidy appearance? Do I cling to material objects or grab a latté when I'm feeling blue?

God wants me to grow up. Sometimes that means putting away anything I go to for comfort besides Him. This doesn't mean I don't go to my husband or my friends when I need a hug or an encouraging word, but it does mean that I'm not to depend on anyone other than Jesus Christ for my ultimate security.

P.S. I have a secret. I still have Steven's yellow blanket. It's in a cedar chest with other treasures of his childhood. And one day I hope to hand it to another little towheaded child…at least for a season.

44

Old Enough to Learn

Teach me your way, O LORD,
and I will walk in your truth.

PSALM 86:11

The little girl bounced up and down, trying to see over the counter at the bank as her daddy made a deposit. She was about three feet tall and not quite big enough to get a clear view.

"How old are you?" the teller asked.

The little girl stood up straight and said, "I'm four years old, and next year I'm going to be five, and then I'll be old enough to learn."

Of course she'd been learning her entire life. Being five just meant she could go to school.

Then God reminded me that sometimes we put off learning about Him until...well, later. When the kids go off to school. When I finish this big project. When I retire. But the time for learning about God is *now.* All day God speaks to us through creation, other people, and our circumstances, but the most important way we learn about Him is through the pages of the Bible. He has written us an incredible love letter filled with precious promises, comforting commands, and godly guildelines just waiting to be discovered. We're never too old or too young to learn.

45

A Child's Faith

A little child will lead them.

ISAIAH 11:6

"And dear God," my little boy whispered, "I pray that you give Mommy and Daddy another Jaynes baby."

After four years of praying for God to bless us with a second child, we realized that might not be His plan for our family. However, every night my little boy, Steven, prayed for another "Jaynes baby." But how do you tell someone to stop praying a prayer?

As I pondered this dilemma, God took care of it for me. Just before his fifth birthday Steven and I were sitting at his child-sized table eating peanut butter and jelly sandwiches. He looked up at me, and with all the wisdom of the prophets asked, "Mommy, have you ever thought that God might want you to have only *one* Jaynes baby?"

"Yes, son, I have," I said. "And if that's the case, I'm glad He gave me everything I ever wanted in one package when He gave me you."

"Well, what I think we ought to do is to pray until you're too old to have one. Then we'll know that was His answer."

Steven had no idea how old "too old" was. He knew Sarah in the Bible was 90 when she delivered Isaac. But whatever the outcome, Steven wasn't having a problem with God saying no. My son knew I said no to him many times, and no didn't mean "I don't love you." Rather it meant "I'm your parent, and I know what's best for you."

God taught me a great lesson that day. Through Steven's childlike faith, God gave me an example of the attitude of trust I should have toward my heavenly Father who loves me and knows what's best for me…and sometimes that means accepting when His answer is no.

46

Forgiving Karl

Forgive as the Lord forgave you.
COLOSSIANS 3:13

Eighteen-year-old Karl stood before the court a broken young man. Seven months earlier this graduate from Camden Military Academy and some friends had a party with a keg of beer. Late in the night he and his best friend, Wayne, jumped into a Jeep. Karl was at the wheel. The car rounded a curve and drifted left. Karl overcorrected and cut a hard right. Then he cut back to the left again. The right tires blew and the rims dug into the road. The Jeep flipped and ejected Wayne some 50 feet, and he landed on the pavement in the middle of the road. Karl remained in the Jeep, but he was badly injured. For the first time he realized he might be drunk.

The tranquility of the night was pierced by sirens, a rescue helicopter, and wailing young adults. Six days later Wayne Campbell, the only son of Trish Campbell, died.

Karl stood before the court to await his sentence.

Person after person spoke on his behalf. But it was Wayne's mother who surprised us all.

"My son and Karl went to school together and were best friends," she began. "I love this boy like he was my own child. It is not my wish that he should serve prison time. I understand that he has to have some type of punishment, but I know Karl is truly remorseful and never intended this to happen.

"I am a sinner and God sent His only Son to save me and forgive me of my sins. I'm not worthy of that forgiveness. So why wouldn't I forgive Karl?"

For those watching, the act wasn't human—it was divine.

Amazing grace, how sweet the sound.

47

A Dirty Story with a Sweet Ending

Ask and you will receive.
JOHN 16:24

teve and I built a home on some of the rockiest soil in the county, and we were going to have to haul in truckloads of dirt in order to plant grass. But I struggled with the idea of paying for dirt.

A few days later I was driving down my street and noticed a crew of men digging a huge trench to install a waterline. I slowed down, and there before me stood a beautiful sight: piles and piles of dirt.

One of the flagmen stopped me as a dump truck blocked the road. While my car was idling my mind was in overdrive. It was as if God said to me, "Okay, girl, tell Me what you see."

"I see a big bulldozer, a dump truck, and a pot-bellied man who probably likes to eat holding up a stop sign."

"Sir," I said in my sweetest Southern drawl through

my opened window, "what are you going to do with that dirt?"

"Just dump it somewhere," he said.

"I'll tell you what," I said. "You dump that dirt in my yard, and I'll make you and your men a chocolate pie every day you're here."

I could almost see his buttons getting tighter with visions of delicious pastry floating in his head. I had myself a deal.

By the end of the summer I had a small mountain range of beautiful rich soil in my front yard, and the construction crew had a few extra pounds around their waists.

The Bible says the Proverbs 31 woman saw a field and bought it. I guess I did it one truckload at a time.

48

Chosen

In him we were also chosen.
EPHESIANS 1:11

K.C. was a beautiful blonde freshman at Georgia State University. She was excited to be at college and looked forward to having a fresh start at life. When "rush" week came around, she was the first to sign up. This was the week when all the young women who desired to become members of sororities went from Greek house to Greek house, mingling and hoping to be chosen to become a "sister." After the tiring week of parties, constant smiling, and small talk, the young adults waited anxiously for the Friday night party to find out who had chosen them. K.C. was getting dressed for the celebration when the phone rang.

"Hello," K.C. answered cheerfully.

"Hi, K.C., this is Cassie, the rush coordinator. I'm sorry to tell you this, but looking at the list, no one chose you."

Those words, "No one chose you," rang in K.C.'s ears for years.

I spoke at a conference about our new identity in Christ, and K.C. came up afterward and told me this story. She'd never told anyone before, but now she was free from the pain of those words.

"For the first time in my life, I can let go of that pain because I realize I *was* chosen. God chose me. He chose *me*. So what if those sorority girls didn't. God chose me, and that's much more impressive than a sorority pin."

And God chose you, precious friend! Like a groom who chooses, pursues, and captures the love of his life, He chose you.

49

Trick Skis

*When they measure themselves by themselves and
compare themselves with themselves, they are not wise.*

2 CORINTHIANS 10:12

"Slow down!" I yelled as Steve barreled down
the snow-covered mountain.

When I taught my husband to snow ski, he
learned to slow down by turning his skis to the left
or right. However, he had a tendency to turn too
far, and he'd end up with the tip of his skis pointing
up the hill. Inevitably gravity would take its course,
and he would slide down the hill backward. Eventually he discovered that if he simply continued the
turn, making a complete circle, he would indeed slow
down and keep from going downhill backward. It
was a sight to behold as Steve spiraled down the
mountain, making giant circles in the snow.

Toward the end of the day a woman approached
Steve and asked, "Sir, I have been watching your
beautiful acrobatics all day long. Can you teach me
how to make those wonderful circles in the snow?"

Steve laughed and obliged.

Isn't that the way life is? Sometimes we look at other people and think they "have it all together." *Oh, if I could just handle life the way she does,* we muse. *If I just had an orderly house like her, well-mannered children like her, a loving husband like her.* In reality, she is most likely going in circles, just like you are, doing whatever it takes not to go downhill the wrong way.

But if we take our eyes off other people and keep them focused on God, our paths will be straight. And hopefully, when someone asks, "Can you show me how to depend on God like you do?" we'll be able to oblige.

50

Swollen Imaginations

*Finally, brothers and sisters, whatever
is true...think about such things.*
PHILIPPIANS 4:8 (TNIV)

*A*da sat down in the dental chair as if every move took great effort. She could barely open her mouth to let the dentist (my husband) see what the problem might be. Finally she parted her lips ever so slightly, and Steve gingerly lifted her lip. A grin spread across his face as he reached in and removed a small cotton roll from the area between her cheek and tooth.

Ada's eyes popped wide open as she bolted upright in the chair. "What did you do?" she said, all signs of weakness gone. She was suddenly healed!

"This was left in your mouth from yesterday's procedure," Steve said as he held up a small cotton roll. "This is what was causing you so much pain."

The day before, Steve had placed a filling in Ada's tooth. He put a cotton roll between her cheek and tooth to keep it dry, and his humble assistant (me) forgot to take it out. When Ada got home and the numbness wore off, she felt her "swollen" cheek and thought the worst. As the night wore on, she worked herself into a tizzy and could barely raise her head. Never once did she open her mouth and look inside. Her imagination wreaked havoc, and she could barely walk or hold her head up. Now she hung her head for a different reason—embarrassment.

God reminded me that sometimes I do the very same thing. I let a tiny splinter of deception fester until my emotions become infected with the lie. If I close my eyes I can almost see God pulling out the perceived cause of pain and saying, "Is this what's bothering you?"

Then I realize everything really is okay.

51

Bushwhacked

*Every branch that does bear fruit he prunes
so that it will be even more fruitful.*

JOHN 15:1

"Honey, it's time to cut the bushes back," my husband announced.

After 10 years, our lush bushes were at their peak of fullness and beauty. And now my husband planned on cutting them back? To bare branches? No way!

"Sharon, they look great on the outside," he said, "but inside they're bare. Cutting them back so the sun can reach the inside will make them healthier and fuller in the long run."

Reluctantly, I submitted to Rambo and his hedge trimmer as he bushwhacked my beautiful shrubs. The bushes looked like shaved dogs standing sentinel around our house. They seemed almost embarrassed, standing naked and bare. However, in about two months little green leaves began to emerge from the remaining branches, and within a few more weeks the bushes were healthy and more beautiful than before.

Through that process, God showed me that sometimes I need a good trimming. I can get so involved in ministry and life that my insides grow a bit bare. I might look spiritually healthy on the outside, but on the inside, where it really counts, I may be languishing...sometimes without even knowing it. So God comes along with His holy hedge trimmers and begins lopping off the beautiful branches.

"What are You doing?" I cry.

"Don't worry," He says. "You'll feel bare for a time, but in the end you'll be even healthier and more spiritually beautiful than before."

I've grown accustomed to Steve and his dogged determination to cut the bushes back. And I've grown accustomed to God's perfect pruning in my life as well.

52

Barking! Barking! Barking!

*Let us fix our eyes on Jesus, the author
and perfecter of our faith.*
HEBREWS 12:2

When I take my routine walk through the neighborhood, I'm always accompanied by a wave of barking dogs indignant that I dare pass by their turf. I try not to let it hurt my feelings, but it's never ceased to unnerve me. I wish the pups would wag their tails as I walk by, as if to say, "Oh, there's that sweet Mrs. Jaynes. My how I like her. I wish she were my master, and we could take walks together. Mrs. Jaynes! Mrs. Jaynes, won't you please come over and pat my head?" But for 20 years, it's always growl, ruff, and bark.

I hate to admit it, but it's been the same way in my spiritual journey from time to time. I've heard some unfriendly barking, some disapproving snarling, and a few disdainful growls. But in the midst of the clamor God is walking alongside me as well:

> *I love you, My precious child. I love walking with you. I see your efforts to follow Me, and I have provided a great cloud of witnesses to cheer you on. Your name is written in the palm of My hand—not so I won't forget it, but because I have held you so tightly, you have left a lasting impression there. Keep walking. You're doing well. Focus on the cheers and not the jeers.*

There will always be those who voice their disapproval as we walk life's path. But if we listen carefully, we can hear the gentle voice of God encouraging us to press on.

53

Alarming News

For God does not show favoritism.
ROMANS 2:11

"Are you the owners of this building?" the neighbor demanded as we put the finishing touches on Steve's new office.

"Yes. May I help you?" Steve said.

"I certainly hope so. Your alarm system keeps going off in the middle of the night and waking up my grandson. I want it to stop."

"I'm so sorry," Steve said. "The security system goes off at the slightest vibration. The company is supposed to come by on Monday to adjust it. Until then, we'll keep it turned off."

"Thanks, I'd appreciate that," the man said as he walked out of the building.

Our painter, standing on a ladder, held his paintbrush in midair with a look of terror on his face.

"What's wrong?" I asked him.

"Ma'am, do you know who that was?" he asked.

"Yes, I do. He's a prominent evangelist in this town."

"I wouldn't make that guy mad. He's got a direct line to God!"

I laughed and said, "Oh, honey, don't worry about that. I've got a direct line too!"

The painter looked alarmed.

"As a matter-of-fact, you can have one too. Whether you're a painter, a preacher, a homemaker, or a doctor, the ground is level at the foot of the cross, and we all can have direct access to God. All you have to do is pray. He'll listen."

As the painter continued to change the hue of the wall, I could see God changing the attitude of his heart. God became the painter on the palette of the man's soul with broad brushstrokes of love and acceptance that the worker had never considered before.

54

Who's the Boss?

This is love for God: to obey his commands.
1 JOHN 5:3

"No," he said when I asked him to put on his coat. "No," he responded when I told him to take a bath. "No," he said when I told him to wash his hands.

For two months Alex, a ten-year-old foreign exchange student from Russia, became part of our family. While his mastery of English was scant, his use of *no* was prolific. Whether it was "Alex, take a bath," "Alex, comb your hair," or "Alex, eat your breakfast," I was met with a stern-faced "no." However, my job was to teach him that in America, parents are the bosses, or at least they should be, so I simply kept repeating my request until I wore him down and he complied.

Two months after his arrival, Alex flew back home with new clothes, new shoes, and other new American merchandise. I'm not sure how much he learned about the American Christian family, but I learned a great deal about the word *no*.

When a two-year-old looks you in the eye, plants his feet, and puckers up his sweet little cherub lips to form the word *no*, it's almost comical. But when a ten-year-old looks you straight in the eye and forms that same word, it's no longer cute.

The foreign exchange student experience turned out to be quite an education…for me. I discovered the frustration God must feel when we plant our feet, with our hands on our hips, and say "no" to Him. How foolish we are to refuse our loving Parent's commands! But hopefully He'll keep repeating the commands until we figure out that He's the Boss.

55

Aliens and Strangers

Our citizenship is in heaven.
PHILIPPIANS 3:20

*A*lex, our Russian exchange student, had a very limited understanding of English, and we were dependent on hand signals and facial expressions to get by. I tried once to get him to write his parents a letter. I pulled out the stationery, handed him a pen, pointed to a picture of his parents, and said, "Why don't we write your parents a letter?"

He had no idea what I was talking about.

For 20 minutes I drew pictures and tried to get him to understand. Finally, with tears in his eyes, he looked up at me and said, "What do?"

I just hugged him and put the pen and paper away.

Sometimes I feel just like our little Russian guest. I don't understand the cruelty I read in the papers and hear on the news. I'm confused at the angry attitudes of drivers with road rage. I don't understand how an adult could harm a child. In confusion I look to my heavenly Father and say, "What do?"

He reminds me that we will never feel at home here on earth. We are aliens, foreigners, strangers just passing through. Our true citizenship is in heaven, and we're just foreign exchange students here for a short while.

We're not home yet.

56

Mining for Gold

When he has tested me, I will come forth as gold.

JOB 23:10

I knelt beside the creek bed surrounded by 30 fourth graders panning for gold. We were at Reid Gold Mine, and I was the chaperone of the rowdy young miners. The tour guide took us through dark musty tunnels, explaining how the miners a hundred years ago searched for veins of gold embedded in the rocks and hidden beneath the sodden walls. Many tirelessly panned for gold in the mountain stream in hopes of finding a few valuable nuggets.

After the tour we each grabbed a sieve and tried our luck. First we lowered pans into the mud of the streambed and filled our sieves. Then we shook the sieves back and forth, allowing the crystal clear water to flow over its contents. The silt filtered through the screen and fell back into the stream as hopeful children (and a few adults) searched for gold. Unfortunately none of us struck it rich that day, but I did discover a valuable treasure.

As I filled my sieve with mud, I saw a reflection of my life filled with filth and pain. Then, as I shook the bowl back and forth, the cool, pure water of God's Spirit washed over me. I imagined God washing through my memories and the dirt falling to the ground, leaving nuggets of gold behind.

Our lives, no matter how messy, are filled with gold nuggets. We need to look beyond the dirt and allow God to expose the treasures just waiting to be discovered.

57

A Dainty Morsel

*The perverse stir up dissension,
and gossips separate close friends.*
PROVERBS 16:28 (TNIV)

monster was sneaking into my yard in the dark of night and devouring my prize flowers. I never saw his beady eyes or heard his pounding footsteps—just the aftermath of his destruction. He left a trail of slime as he moved from plant to plant, leaving gaping holes in broadleaf gerbera daisies, gnawing entire velvety purple petunia blossoms, and reducing bushy begonias to naked stalks.

I asked a neighbor about my flowerbed's demise, and she determined, "You've got slugs."

"Slugs!" I exclaimed. "The yard monster is a tiny slug?"

"You can put out slug bait to catch them and see for yourself," she said.

I sprinkled slug bait all around the yard and then waited. The next morning I viewed the "monster" remains. The beasts were a quarter inch long—about the size of my little toenail.

How could something so small cause so much damage in such a short amount of time? I wondered. Suddenly I thought of something else that is very small but can cause enormous damage in a short amount of time: gossip. King Solomon wrote, "The words of a gossip are like choice morsels; they go down to a man's inmost parts" (Proverbs 18:8). Just as one tiny slug can destroy a flowerbed, so one tiny morsel of gossip can destroy a person's reputation, mar someone's character, and devour a friendship.

I never did get rid of all the slugs. And even though I never see them in the daytime, I can always tell where they've been by the slimy trail of destruction they leave behind.

58

Foot Holding

*My grace is sufficient for you, for my
power is made perfect in weakness.*

2 CORINTHIANS 12:9

Something strange was going on in my head, and the doctors couldn't figure out what it was. "You'll need an MRI," the doctor decided. "Are you claustrophobic?"

I assured him I was not.

The day of the exam, a nurse strapped me on a table, taped my head down on both sides, and pushed a button that slid me into a metal tube like a hotdog in a bun. Suddenly I couldn't breathe.

"Take me out!" I yelled.

"You're having a panic attack," she said after I slid out.

"I am not! Try it again." But each time I met the same fate.

"You'll have to come back another day," she finally said.

All my life I've conquered the impossible. And

what is so hard about being in a metal tube for 45 minutes? I went home and told my friend Mary Ruth about my ordeal.

"I feel like such a weenie," I confessed.

"That's baloney," she said. "You just need a friend. We'll do this together."

The next week I went back with my secret weapon (Mary Ruth). She stood at the end of the tube, held my foot, prayed, and waved like Howdy Doody. The procedure went off without a hitch.

All my life I've struggled with wanting to be self-sufficient, but through extraordinary moments like these God reminds me, "My grace is sufficient for you, for my power is made perfect in weakness." It's okay to be weak. It's more than okay; it's His plan. When we admit that we are weak, He gives us His strength.

Many times God pumps courage into us through a friend who holds our hand. In this case He used Mary Ruth to hold my foot.

59

Acting like a Dog

Even though I was once a blasphemer and a persecutor and a violent man, I was shown mercy because I acted in ignorance and unbelief.

1 TIMOTHY 1:13

Mr. and Mrs. Cottontail decided to start their family under our gazebo, but not everyone in the Jaynes family was happy about it. Several times I caught Ginger, our golden retriever, pawing at the dirt around the gazebo, trying her best to get to them.

"No, Ginger," I scolded. "Get away from there!"

One day as I worked in the yard, one of the baby bunnies ventured out from under her safe haven. Ginger grabbed it quicker than I could say "jackrabbit."

"Steve!" I screamed. "Ginger's got a bunny!"

Steve grabbed Ginger and gently took the bunny from her mouth. "I think she broke its legs," he said.

"I'm so mad at Ginger!" I said. "I'm not sure I want a dog that would hurt a bunny."

"Sharon, you can't get mad at a dog for acting like a dog."

Later that evening I had an extraordinary moment with God as I replayed the scene in my mind. Steve was right—I shouldn't get mad at a dog for acting like a dog. Likewise, I shouldn't get mad at someone who doesn't know Jesus for acting like someone who doesn't know Jesus. It's a common mistake, but one that Ginger—and God—taught me well.

60

Consider the Puppies

Consider how the lilies grow. They do not labor
or spin. Yet I tell you, not even Solomon in all
his splendor was dressed like one of these.

LUKE 12:27

She rhythmically panted, held her breath, and pushed—unsure about what was happening to her body yet instinctively cooperating with each contraction. When the first puppy was born, Ginger took one look at that wet, mousy creature and sprang into action. She chewed the umbilical cord to one-half inch from the puppy's tummy and then began licking life into its motionless body. In just a few minutes Fletcher, her firstborn, scootched around, rooting for his mother's milk. Once again Ginger knew exactly what to do. Satisfied, she looked up at me and smiled. (Well, it looked like a smile to me.)

About two hours later she started the now familiar panting again, and puppy number two entered the world. When number three emerged, she was still in the amniotic sac, floating like a ragdoll in a ziplock bag. Ginger chewed a hole in the sac and pulled the puppy out. When she realized it wasn't breathing, she licked more vigorously than before until the pup started breathing on its own. For six hours I watched in amazement as Ginger performed one miraculous feat after another. No one taught her what to do; God had placed the "knowing" in her.

The delivery birthed a whole new appreciation of the love and care God has for all of His creation. And if He cares that much for puppies, consider how much more He cares for you and me...we who are created in His very image.

61

I Quit!

At just the right time we will reap a
harvest of blessing if we don't give up.
GALATIANS 6:9 (NLT)

quit!" Steven threw his bicycle on the ground,
placed his balled up fists on his four-year-old
hips, and kicked the rear tire.

For several hours he'd been trying to ride his bike
without training wheels. Each time he tried, he lost
his balance and fell to the ground.

"I can't do it!" he stormed.

"You can't do it *yet*," I corrected. "But you will.
And when you learn to ride your bike, it will be the
funnest thing you do as a kid."

Steven looked me in the eye. "This is not fun, and
it will never be fun."

Oh my, how I saw myself in those eyes. So many
times when God is trying to teach me a life lesson
or a new discipline I lose my balance and want to
quit. He takes the training wheels off and sets me on
the road of maturity, and sometimes I tumble to the

ground. "I can't do it!" I cry. "This is not fun, and it will never be fun."

But God just keeps on working with me, holding the back of the bicycle until I learn to balance and keep moving straight ahead. The next thing I know, I'm cruising down victory lane, and God is laughing with delight.

A few days after Steven's declaration of defeat, he walked out the door, hopped on his little red bike, and pedaled around the yard without losing his balance once. And you know what? Riding his bicycle *was* the funnest thing he ever did as a kid.

62

An Opening in the Clouds

*The men were amazed and asked,
"What kind of man is this? Even the
winds and the waves obey him!"*

MATTHEW 8:27

We'd been circling over the small airport in Texas for 25 minutes, and I wondered just how long the fuel was going to last.

I was on my way to speak to a group of ladies at a weekend retreat. We were just about to land when the pilot announced over the loudspeaker that a terrible storm was making visibility impossible to touch down. So we circled and circled and circled. Finally he came back on and informed us that he'd found an opening in the clouds and was going to "give it a try."

Give it a try! I didn't like the sound of that.

I'm happy to report that we landed safely. As a matter-of-fact, we were the *only* plane to land at that airport that evening. Every other flight turned around and headed back to Dallas.

As I walked off the airplane I realized that many people are like planes caught in a storm. During difficult times some people circle for days, weeks, or years, afraid to land and get on with life. Some people turn around and run from the storm, never getting where God intended. And some people are so afraid they never board the flight in the first place. It's the rare few who ask God to part the clouds so they can land on solid ground.

I'm glad the pilot "gave it a try." I wouldn't have wanted it any other way.

63

Preparing for Baby

In my Father's house are many rooms; if it were not so, I would have told you. I am going there to prepare a place for you.

JOHN 14:2

arrie set the brightly wrapped package on her bulging tummy and plucked the pastel bow from its lid. Everyone at the baby shower oohed and aahed as she held up an infant's pink terrycloth sleeper with tiny snaps and bootie feet. It was hard to believe that in just a few short weeks her first child would be filling that tiny outfit.

When a baby is snuggled in a mother's womb, he has no idea the commotion and excitement that surrounds the grand debut. The nursery is prepared down to the most minute detail, including a rocking chair waiting expectantly in the corner, a crib with a dancing mobile of elephants on parade, a music box ready to chime *It's a Small World,* and a changing table with all the modern paraphernalia to keep bottoms dry. Then there's the painting and the sewing and the...well, the list is endless. No, a baby in the womb has no idea the preparations that are taking place or just how much love awaits his or her arrival.

I wonder if that's how God feels about us. The Bible tells us that He is preparing a room for us, and I imagine our heavenly Father is crafting each and every detail to perfection. And just as a baby has no idea how much love awaits him as he passes from the safe haven of his mother's womb into her embracing arms, we have no idea just how much love awaits us as we pass from this temporary dwelling place into our eternal home.

64

What Kind of Friend Are You?

*Let us consider how we may spur one
another on toward love and good deeds.*

HEBREWS 10:24

*I*t was an accidental experiment. Sometimes those
are the best kind.

I sent out an on-line devotion before my husband had a chance to proofread it. I have trouble
finding my own errors because I know what I meant
to say. (That's a lesson in itself. Just think on that a
moment.) When I re-read the posted devotion later,
I was horrified. It was smattered with typos and mistakes. *Oh well,* I thought as I humbly clicked delete.
Grace, grace, grace.

Then the comments from readers began to arrive.

"Check your spelling! Run a grammar check!" one
woman wrote.

"Today's devotion meant so much to me," another
said. "Thank you for ministering to me."

One person wrote, "Sharon, I just hate to see typos in your wonderful devotions. I know you're busy. Why don't you send them to me, and I will proof them for you?"

Then I had an extraordinary moment with God. He showed me three types of friends represented by the comments:

- One woman pointed out my faults.

- One woman overlooked my faults and encouraged me in the ways I had blessed her.

- One woman encouraged me, acknowledged my errors, and then went one step further by offering to help.

Then God asked me, "What kind of friend do you want to be?"

65

The Look of Love

Do not be afraid; you will not suffer shame...
You will forget the shame of your youth.

ISAIAH 54:4

er invisible cloak of shame was so heavy it drug on the ground behind her and weighed down her petite shoulders. Hidden beneath her chocolate eyes and beautiful smile was a secret that bore down on her heart. She tried to blink back tears, but they spilled down her peach-like cheeks.

"Gina, do you want to talk about it?" I asked.

"I'm so ashamed!" she cried. "I want to tell someone, but I'm afraid. I've never told anyone before."

For the next hour or so Gina poured out her story of fleeing the advances of her stepfather, living on the street, and engaging in prostitution at the urging of a woman who said she cared.

"Every time I did it, a part of me died," she said. "I didn't do it for long, but I've never been able to forget the shame and how dirty I felt. Even though I'm now married, have two children, and a wonderful life, I still feel dirty. It was a long time ago, but it feels like yesterday. Nobody knows—not even my husband. He always tells me how precious I am. If he knew, it would kill him."

We talked for a long time about God's forgiveness and the clean slate He offers us at the cross. Gina knew most of that in her head, but her heart was having trouble believing it could be so easy.

After we talked I asked, "Are you glad you told me?"

"Yes. Mainly because the way you're looking at me now is not any different than the way you were looking at me before you knew."

And that's the truth of grace.

66

When You Least Expect It

We are not unaware of [Satan's] schemes.
2 CORINTHIANS 2:11

On Tuesday morning, September 11, 2001, after I got my son off to school and my husband off to work, I took a long walk through the neighborhood. The sky was crystal clear with a gentle breeze rustling the orange and yellows of the newly changing leaves. There was nothing special on my schedule—just the ordinary. However, one hour later, the day turned into anything but ordinary. I watched in horror as the television played and replayed the airplanes crashing into the World Trade Center towers and the Pentagon.

"O God," I prayed, "we never saw it coming."

That's always how the enemy attacks, He seemed to say, *when you least expect it.*

My mind raced back to December 31, 1999, the day the world braced itself for the potentially disastrous effects of Y2K. Families and businesses alike prepared for months for what might occur as the clock ticked past 11:59 P.M. We held our breaths, clasped our hands, and braced ourselves. Yes, we were ready...and nothing happened. The new millennium came without incident.

Do you see the correlation? There is an enemy who seeks to steal, kill, and destroy (John 10:10). His name is Satan, and he desires to destroy us just as the hijackers destroyed the Twin Towers. And our first line of defense is to be prepared. To be ready. To anticipate his attacks and be on the alert.

67

The Power of the Truth

You will know the truth, and the truth will set you free.
JOHN 8:32

Hollywood was coming to town! The city was all abuzz as the movie cameras rolled in to film *The Patriot*, starring Mel Gibson as Benjamin Martin. Several of my neighbors excitedly tried out to be stand-ins or extras. We were thrilled when the directors chose my little nine-year-old neighbor, Michael. He was to be the stand-in for Benjamin Martin's son, Samuel. For months Michael wore his long hair with extensions, slipped on Italian knickers and knee-high stockings, and acted the part of an American colonial boy. He traveled to rural South Carolina where part of the movie was taped and received an education in productions for the silver screen. Michael saw how producers and makeup artists made something appear as though it was real when it wasn't.

The movie was a bloody, realistic reenactment of the horrors of the Revolutionary War. During one scene Mel Gibson pummeled a British soldier and landed a hatchet squarely in the middle of his forehead. I covered my eyes in horror as Michael watched unmoved.

"Mrs. Jaynes, that's not real," he said. "That guy walked around the set with that hatchet in his head for three days. We even ate lunch together, and he had that hatchet with fake blood glued to his face. It's not real."

Then God reminded me of the attitude I should have when the enemy tries to steal my faith and turn it to fear with his lies. *That's not real. Big deal!*

Michael knew what was true, and it removed his fear. That's the power of truth.

68

Thank You, Lord, for My Dirty Floor

I will bless the LORD at all times;
His praise shall continually be in my mouth.
PSALM 34:1 (NASB)

I'm so tired of mopping this kitchen floor," I grumbled. "Does anyone even notice all my hard work? And besides, they're just going to come in here and dirty it all up again anyway."

I was in a less than cheerful mood and complained with each swipe of my mop. Then God posed a few questions:

- *Suppose you were blind and couldn't see the beautiful patterns on the linoleum floor or the spilled juice by the refrigerator or the crumbs under the baby's chair?*

- *What if you were deaf? You couldn't hear the soothing sound of the soap bubbles dissolving in the scrub bucket or the rhythmic sound of the mop being pushed back and forth across the floor's hard surface.*

- *Suppose you were in a wheelchair and not strong enough to stand and grasp the mop handle?*
- *What if you didn't have a home or a family to clean up after?*

Suddenly God mopped up my attitude, and I began to pray, "Thank You, Lord, for the privilege of mopping this dirty floor. Thank You for the health and the strength to hold this mop, for the ability to wrap my fingers around its handle and feel the wood in my hands. Thank You for the sight to see the crumbs and the dirt and for the sense of smell to enjoy the clean scent of the soap in my bucket. Thank You for the many precious feet that will walk through this room and dirty it up again. And Lord, thank You for the privilege of having a floor to mop and a family to clean up after."

69

The Work of Art

I praise you because I am fearfully
and wonderfully made;
your works are wonderful,
I know that full well.

PSALM 139:14

*I*t was truly a work of art. Yes, one eye was much larger than the other, the nose resembled a giant squash, and the ears looked like saucers on the side of his head. But my son's kindergarten self-portrait unveiled on parents night is a masterpiece I've treasured throughout the years.

Steven's drawing had a striking resemblance to some works by world-renowned Picasso. However, Picasso's paintings are worth millions of dollars and my son's are valuable only to me. Why the difference? The value is based on the artist who created it.

Ah, it was an extraordinary moment with God when I realized the reason for *my* great value was because of the Artist who created me. He meticulously created my inmost being, curiously knit me together in my mother's womb, and intricately wove me together with various colors and hues. Just as a masterpiece exists in the mind of the creator, God saw my unformed substance before the weaving began.

Steven's masterpiece still hangs in my home today. And you and I are living works of art on display in God's universal gallery.

70

Help Me, Lord!

O LORD, come quickly to help me.
PSALM 40:13

"Get it out! Get it out!" Steven cried as he held his hand over his eye. He was eight years old at the time and had been playing on the swing set when a piece of bark flew into his eye.

"Get it out!" he cried as he ran into the house.

"Son, you're going to have to take your hand away if you want me to get it out."

"No! Don't touch it!"

Steven went back and forth between "get it out" and "don't touch it" for about 45 minutes. Finally the pain overcame his fear, and he decided to trust me. It took 45 minutes for me to convince him to remove his hand and 30 seconds for me to remove the piece of bark from his eye.

As he ran back out into the yard to play, I saw myself in Steven's struggle. So many times I cry out to God, "Get it out! Get it out!" I desperately want Him to take care of a problem that's causing me pain, and yet at the same time I hold on to it so tightly He can't. What I saw in this earthly struggle between parent and child was a reflection of the heavenly struggle God must have with me sometimes.

I can almost hear God now: "Sharon, you're going to have to take your hand away if you want Me to take care of the problem."

Kids...they can be so stubborn at times.

71

Lost and Found

*The Son of Man came to seek and
to save what was lost.*

LUKE 19:10

*I*t was our first trip to Disney World, and my video
camera was poised to capture precious memories.
But the video didn't start out as I'd planned. As it
begins, we're in a welcoming center where children
are climbing on various objects, crawling through
tunnels, and swinging from monkey bars. Then I
see my husband running toward the camera, his face
growing larger and larger until it fills the frame.

"Where's Steven?" he cries. "I can't find him any-
where!"

Then the screen goes blank.

What a way to start our vacation! Steven had
wandered away, climbed into one of those tunnels,
and had yet to emerge. We panicked. Who wants
to lose their kid at Disney World? Of course, we did
find him.

He had no idea he was even lost.

Ah, did that last sentence give you pause?

Even as I wrote it, God quickly reminded me that I was in the same situation. I had no idea I was lost, but my heavenly Father found me.

After Adam and Eve disobeyed God in the Garden of Eden, they hid from Him. When He came looking for them in the cool of the evening, He asked the first question recorded in the Bible: *Where are you?* That question runs like a scarlet thread from Genesis through Revelation.

So where are you? No matter what you've done, no matter how far you've strayed from God's perfect plan for your life, He is always in pursuit of you. All you have to do is come out from hiding and say, "Here I am, Lord."

72

Some Things Never Change

I the LORD do not change.
MALACHI 3:6

*I*n this ever-changing world, my husband has been a constant rock in my life. He is even-tempered and wonderfully predictable. In his office he has seven female employees with seven sets of percolating hormones. As I listened to his stories and sensed his frustration in trying to understand each woman on any given day, I had visions of *Dr. Snow White and the Seven Dwarfs.* I suggested he put the names Doc, Bashful, Happy, Sleepy, Sneezy, Dopey, and Grumpy in a basket and let each woman choose the name that describes how she's feeling that day. It would take the guesswork out of knowing how they were for Steve, and he would know how to better respond to each one. Of course at the end of the day, he would have to put the names back in the basket and bring them home so I could pick out my mood du jour.

Aren't you glad God never changes? He is always faithful, righteous, holy, loving, all-powerful, all-knowing, and all-present. He is Jehovah-jireh, the Lord who provides; Jehovah-rapha, the Lord who heals; Jehovah-shalom, the Lord our peace; Jehovah-shammah, the Lord who is there; Jehovah-raah, the Lord my Shepherd; and Jehovah-sabaoth, the Lord of Hosts.

What a comfort to know that we don't serve a God who is ever-changing like we are. He is the same "yesterday, today, and forever."

73

Three Squirrels

*He who began a good work in you will carry it
on to completion until the day of Christ Jesus.*

PHILIPPIANS 1:6

The squirrels were driving me mad. I love birds, but as soon as I'd fill up a birdfeeder, squirrels arrived on cue and emptied it. They'd hang upside down by one grubby paw while seemingly waving at me with the other. And for some reason there were always three of them. I tried various contraptions to keep them at bay, but they always figured out a way to overcome the obstacles. They'd find a way over it, under it, around it, or even sit on it.

Finally I resorted to a squirrel cage to capture the furry varmints and release them in a distant field. The first day I set the bait (birdseed, of course), caught all three squirrels, and released them in the country where they scampered away.

You can imagine my horror when I arose the next morning to look out at the birdfeeder and saw squirrels—three of them! On the second day I captured

three more squirrels and took them to the country...
and the third day, and the fourth day. For every three
squirrels I took to the country, three more showed
up the next day.

I returned the cage to my neighbor. She was
expecting me.

The critters reminded me of the squirrelly attitudes, behaviors, and thoughts I've tried to eradicate.
It seems that just as soon as I have victory in one
area, God shows me another that needs to be captured as well.

I gave up on the squirrels, but I'm so thankful
God will never give up on me!

74

Beggar No More

Now if we are children, then we are heirs—
heirs of God and co-heirs with Christ.

ROMANS 8:17

Dave and Bonnie read about the overcrowded orphanages in Eastern Europe, and God stirred their hearts to adopt not one, two, or three, but four little boys. Foreign adoptions are costly, but the Jacobs had been richly blessed and money was not a problem. After 11 months and miles of red tape, the adoption process was complete, the couple traveled across the ocean to gather their new family.

The flight home took ten hours, so when they arrived at the Atlanta airport for a two-hour layover, they let the rambunctious boys run around the terminal to work out some of their energy. Of course, they never let their new sons out of their sight. After a short while Dave noticed one of the boys watching a man drinking at a water fountain. Even though the child couldn't speak English, he seemed to be making hand motions and using body language to communicate. Dave watched as the man reached into his pocket and handed a dollar bill to his new son. Even though his son didn't speak the language, he knew how to beg using his eyes, hands, and facial expressions.

The little boy had no idea of the riches that came with his adoption. His every need would be met by his new daddy. And even though he was now part of a family with great wealth, he continued to beg for what was freely his.

And that's your story...and mine. We've been adopted by a heavenly Father who provides everything we need. He owns the cattle on a thousand hills, and we never need to beg again for what God wants to freely give.

75

Be Careful What You Pray

*In the morning I lay my requests before you
and wait in expectation.*

PSALM 5:3

Lord, we thank You for this beautiful summer day, and I ask that Steven and Sharon will see and experience Your creation in a new and fresh way. In Jesus' name, amen."

Steve prayed for God to bless our day before he scurried off to work one balmy summer morning. As soon as he walked out the door, it seemed God got busy answering his prayer. Midmorning I discovered an eyeball-blinking, tongue-hurling lizard in my kitchen. With a swat of the broom, his tail detached while the remainder of his scaly body scurried across the room. More swats followed, and the lizard was finally swept outside.

Later in the afternoon I glanced out the porch window to spy a four-foot black snake basking in the summer sun by the sidewalk steps. His erect head scoped out the area like a periscope on the open sea. A frantic call to a neighbor who was home for lunch brought out hoes, shovels, and excited neighborhood boys to watch the snake's demise.

Emotionally weary from "seeing God's creation in a new and fresh way," I glanced into the backyard as I sat down to dinner with my family, only to discover our golden retriever terrorizing an overstuffed field mouse bounding across the grass.

Where's a snake when you need him? I thought. By the time Steve put the mouse out of his misery, our dinner was ruined.

Exhausted, I turned to Steve and said, "Next time you pray for God to reveal His creation in a 'new and fresh way,' could you please be more specific!"

76

The Stairway

*You are no longer a slave, but a son; and since
you are a son, God has made you also an heir.*

GALATIANS 4:7

*I*magine you've just been informed you have inherited a multilevel mansion equipped with every conceivable treasure. You run up the curving brick sidewalk, throw open the massive oak doors, and excitedly run from room to room on the first floor, hardly believing the good fortune bequeathed to you. However, what you discover are not surroundings fit for royalty but sensible chambers adequately furnished and sparsely decorated.

In the foyer a beautifully carved, winding staircase adorned with plush crimson carpet beckons you to climb to the next level. You consider the steps, look back over your shoulder, and decide, "The lower level's enough for me. Besides, I'm afraid of heights. I'll just stay down here where it's safe."

Unbeknown to you, the upper levels house all your inherited treasures. But you've chosen to stay in the servants' quarters. All that stands between you and the gilded ballroom, chandeliered dining hall, and elaborately appointed bedrooms is the staircase. What keeps you on the ground level? Contentment with mediocrity? Fear of the unknown?

We all have an inheritance from our heavenly Father, but oftentimes we spend our days in the servants' quarters, never climbing the stairs to where the true riches are stored. God longs for us to leave our fears behind and enjoy the riches waiting to be discovered. He has amazing gifts available to those who believe. So leave the servants' quarters and claim the inheritance that is already yours!

77

The Message

*We are not trying to please men but
God, who tests our hearts.*

1 THESSALONIANS 2:4

*I*t was my first speaking engagement at a very large
church, and I was terrified. I overheard a group of
women talking about the speaker who had been at
this event the month before. They used words like
powerful, electric, and *eloquent.*

Satan taunted me. "You should bow out now
before you embarrass yourself. What could you pos-
sibly have to say to minister to those ladies? You're
a nobody."

I knew it was the enemy's lies, but I began to
believe him. He made sense. In order to see what
I would be compared to, I went by the church and
purchased a tape of the previous speaker. I paid my
five dollars, popped the tape into the console, and
braced myself for an hour of power.

Nothing happened.

I fast-forwarded the tape and hit play…nothing.

I flipped the tape over…nothing.

The tape was blank.

At that moment I had an extraordinary moment with God.

> *Sharon, you do not need to hear what My servant said to these people last month. The tape is blank because I don't want you to compare yourself to anyone else. It doesn't matter what he said. I will give you a message for these ladies. I can speak through a prophet, I can speak through a fisherman, and I can speak through a donkey. I gave him a message, and I have given you one as well. Who are you performing for, My child—them or Me? Do not compare yourself to anyone. You are My child, and I'm asking you to speak to an audience of One.*

It was indeed an hour of power. I didn't bother getting my money back for the defective tape. It was exactly what I needed to hear.

78

Apron Strings

Train a child in the way he should go, and
when he is old he will not turn from it.

PROVERBS 22:6

"Mom, I'd like to buy Rosemary a little something for her birthday," Steven said. "Could you help me pick it out?"

I sat at the breakfast table with a lump in my throat as I suddenly realized I was no longer the only girl in my little boy's life. He was 12 years old, and a set of brown eyes and a long dark ponytail had caught his eye. Snip went another apron string, and off we went to purchase the gift.

As Steven moved toward adulthood, I knew I would have to keep those scissors sharp. But it was hard. I wanted to keep him close, but that was not God's plan for my child…or any child.

I wondered if Jesus' mother felt the same way as He approached manhood. Then I remembered a Bible passage about a particular day when Jesus was 12. He exerted His independence and stayed behind during the Passover in Jerusalem while His caravan left for home. When Mary and Joseph realized Jesus was not with the group, they frantically searched for Him. Finally, three days later, they found Jesus back in Jerusalem, sitting among the teachers in the temple.

"Didn't you know I had to be in my Father's house?" He asked his exhausted parents.

If Mary had worn an apron, we probably would have heard a snip.

Cutting those apron strings can be difficult, but when we realize we are merely allowing our children to move with freedom into the life God has designed for them, the strings are easier to cut and the transition easier to bear.

79

Rearview Driving

*One thing I do: Forgetting what is
behind and straining toward what is
ahead, I press on toward the goal.*

PHILIPPIANS 3:13-14

I turned the steering wheel a bit to the right, a bit
to the left, and then back to the right again. *Why
am I having trouble backing down this straight driveway?* I wondered. It was pouring down rain, and I
couldn't lean my head out of the window to back
down Brenda's steep driveway. I had no other choice
but to depend on my rearview mirror, and I wasn't
doing too well. Several times I veered off the driveway and left tire tracks in her soggy grass.

Why is this so hard? I moaned to no one in particular.

Then an unexpected stirring answered. *You're
having trouble because cars aren't meant to be driven
backward…and neither are you.*

Suddenly I saw more in my rearview mirror than
the steep driveway behind me. I began to see the

reason many of us have trouble driving down the road of life—we spend too much time looking in the rearview mirror and not enough time looking straight ahead.

In our spiritual journey, it is beneficial to look back to see where we've been, how far God has brought us, and what He has done in our lives. But if we drive through life spending too much time looking in the rearview mirror at past mistakes, abuses, and failures with cries of "if only," we're in for a heap of trouble.

There is a warning etched onto the glass of my side mirrors: *Objects in mirror are closer than they appear.* This could be interpreted in life as, "Focusing on the past leads to a distorted view of reality." Rearview mirrors are helpful, but if we choose to drive through life looking back instead of keeping our focus forward, we're in for a rough journey.

80

All God's Children

You are all one in Christ Jesus.
GALATIANS 3:28

I was standing in line at an amusement park, anything but amused. The sights and sounds of the people crowded around unnerved me: a glitter-covered teenage girl scantily clad in a bikini top and skin-tight shorts, a nose-pierced and tattooed motorcycle gang member with a skull and crossbones on his leather vest, and three snaggletoothed bumpkins spitting tobacco juice on the asphalt to watch it sizzle.

Then God showed up in line with me.

> *Yes, you look nice in your clean white shorts and neatly tucked T-shirt. But I didn't come only for the sweet smelling and nicely groomed. I came for the smelly shepherd, the uneducated fisherman, and the leprous outcast. I came for the glitter-covered teenager, the nose-pierced gang member, the uneducated mountaineer. They are all my children, and I love each of them.*

Seeing God's creatures in a new light, I began to pray:

> *Dear Lord, whatever pain that young teen has experienced to cause her to dress to draw attention to herself, heal those hurts. May the man with the pierced nose have his heart pierced with the realization of the love of Christ. Fill the mountaineers with the knowledge of Jesus Christ and all spiritual wisdom and understanding. These are my brothers and sisters in Christ...or at least they could be.*

God showed me how much He loves all His children, and I was overjoyed to be among them. I was just about to call us all together for a big group hug when I realized we were at the front of the line and ready to be loaded into the death-defying Gauntlet for the ride of our lives.

No one knew God and I had been on quite a roller-coaster ride together already.

81

Setting Dreams Afloat

*Now to him who is able to do immeasurably more
than all we ask or imagine...to him be glory.*

EPHESIANS 3:20

I suddenly felt like Moses' big sister hiding in the bulrushes, waiting to see if someone was going to pull my "baby" from the alligator-infested Nile. This may tend toward the dramatic, but it describes how I felt when I went to the Christian Booksellers Association Convention to present my first manuscript to various publishers. I wondered if anyone would rescue my baby from the piles of manuscripts floating around the convention. I wondered if anyone would think my baby beautiful and adopt it into their publishing family.

As I prayed, God reminded me of Moses' mother, who prayed for someone to rescue her son as she set him afloat in his tiny ark, and how He answered her prayers beyond all she could have imagined. So I placed my hopes and dreams in a basket and set it adrift among the sea of editors. Then I waited anxiously to see if publishers would think it beautiful.

They did.

Dreams are not meant to be clutched close to our breasts in fear. They're meant to be released to God in prayer. It may be frightening, those first steps of faith, but just as a bird was not made for the nest nor a ship for the harbor, our dreams are not meant to be kept tucked away for safekeeping. They are meant to set sail on the ocean of opportunity for horizons unknown.

Moses' mother had a simple dream—that her son would be *delivered*. God had a bigger dream—that Moses would be a *deliverer*.

Place your dreams into God's hands, and watch Him accomplish more than you ever imagined.

82

Just a Bit of Burlap

Dear friends, let us love one another.

1 JOHN 4:7

It was just a bit of burlap peeking out from underneath the soil, but to Ginger it was something that needed to be unearthed. Our dog spied a corner of fabric that enclosed the root ball of our newly planted maple and dug and dug with all her puppy dog might until the burlap was fully exposed. Of course she gave no thought to the saddened sapling she left toppled on the ground.

Is this what we do to our friends? I wondered. *Do we see a tiny flaw peeking through the surface and dig and dig, flinging dirt in every direction until the flaw is exposed…giving no thought to the friend who is toppled in the process?*

Steve and I gently sat the tree back up and lovingly patted the soil back around its dried out roots. Then, because of its weakened state, we braced it with rope tied to stakes in the ground. I watered the tree daily, not knowing if it was going to recover from the trauma.

To our surprise, the tree survived, grew, and even thrived. Oh, that we would do the same for our toppled brothers and sisters in Christ: stand them back up, reestablish their roots in the love of Christ, hold them up if necessary, and water them daily with prayer.

Thankfully, Ginger left the tree alone after that. After all, she never cared about the tree in the first place.

83

Under Construction

We are God's workmanship.
EPHESIANS 2:10

*L*ike an adolescent boy whose growth spurt leaves him with pants that are too short, ears that are too big, and feet that are too clumsy, our town had a growth spurt that left us with roads that were too narrow, schools that were too small, and neighborhoods that were too crowded. Orange-and-white striped construction cones lined busy streets, and as soon as one project was complete, the cones were moved to another thoroughfare for frustrated drivers to maneuver around.

No one likes road construction. Likewise, I don't know many who enjoy God plopping down construction cones in their lives for a little road work of His own.

It seems I'm always under construction. While I would love to live on Easy Street, I spend a lot of time on the Road to Hard Knocks. I have potholes in my thought life, cracks in my character, and lanes that are too small for the amount of traffic on my to-do list. Then God comes in with His construction crew, and before I know it, orange cones appear and a sign goes up: *Closed for repair*. As soon as construction is complete in one area of my life, He moves on to another and begins again. I like the finished product with its level surface and smooth ride, but I dread the work in progress.

Won't it be wonderful when all the construction work is finally complete? I look forward to the day when I walk through the pearly gates and see glistening streets, paved not with the asphalt of my humanity but with the gold of Christ's glory. And hallelujah! There'll be no construction cones in sight!

84

Facing Fear Head On

Trust in the LORD with all your heart,
And lean not on your own understanding;
In all your ways acknowledge Him,
And He shall direct your paths.

PROVERBS 3:5-6 (NKJV)

The elderly gentleman tried his best to avoid looking at the ladies lingerie as he strolled down the department store aisle. With a sudden interest in girls' sizes two to six-x, he craned his head to the right to shield his eyes from the ladies' unmentionables on the left. But what this Southern gentleman didn't realize was that he was on a collision course with a scantily dressed mannequin in a transparent nightie.

Before I could warn him, he ran smack-dab into the mannequin, knocking her off her feet and into his able arms. With the agility of Superman, he lifted her back onto her stand, straightened up her negligee, and resumed his stroll down the aisle. Only now I noticed a slight grin on his face, a twinkle in his eye, and a bit more spring in his step.

He tangled with what he feared most and came out victorious. He held a beautiful woman in his arms, if only for a moment, and helped her back on her feet. What man wouldn't feel proud.

Through the chuckles, God showed me what happens when I try to avoid a sticky situation by turning my head and pretending it's not there. In order to avoid an embarrassing collision, I need to grab Jesus by the hand, keep my eyes straight ahead, and walk the path (or aisle) He has chosen for me. Then I'll probably have a twinkle in my eye and a little more spring in my step as well.

85

Time with Daddy

Delight yourself in the LORD.
PSALM 37:4

"Let's joust, Daddy!" my two-year-old son yelled as my husband walked through the door.

For eight months this was the typical greeting Steve received when he came home from work each day. We were in the midst of building our dream home, and my spare time was spent making window treatments for the new house. The fabric came on five-foot cardboard tubes that soon became Steven's favorite toys. They were megaphones from which important announcements were made, tunnels for matchbox cars, and most importantly, lances for jousting. Steve jousted tirelessly for months with his little best friend.

Nine years later, in a conversation about the infamous "jousting rods," Steven confessed, "When I was two, I used to have terrible nightmares about those huge cardboard tubes chasing me around the house, trying to get me."

Baffled, I asked, "Why didn't you tell us? Why did you want to continue playing with the tubes if they gave you bad dreams?"

"I guess it was because I loved Dad so much and playing the game with him. It was worth having the scary dreams."

My thoughts immediately went to how much I love my heavenly Father and what I am willing to endure to spend time with Him. Time spent with Him doesn't cause me to have bad dreams, but sometimes I endure a house that's not clean or a project screaming to be completed. That's a nightmare for me. But I've discovered there is no greater joy than spending time with my Abba, my heavenly Daddy.

And you know what? He feels the same way about being with me...and with you.

86

Led Astray

*Do not be misled: "Bad company
corrupts good character."*
1 CORINTHIANS 15:33

$f$letcher was a happy golden retriever who never left the boundaries of his happy home…until the enticing Roxy came along. Fletcher lived a carefree existence in the country with his family, the Prices, romping through the woods, cooling off in the lake, and chasing deer down their mile-long driveway.

Then one day Fletcher was introduced to the enticing Roxy. The Price's neighbors went on vacation and left their dog Roxy in their care. Adam had Eve. Samson had Delilah. Now Fletcher had Roxy.

At first it was a furry flurry of activity as Fletcher and Roxy frolicked in their 30-acre woods, swam in their murky pond, and chased wild animals through the forest. But on the second day of her visit, Roxy bounded down the Prices' driveway with Fletcher in tow. The two dogs disappeared.

Two days later the Prices found the duo muddy, hungry, and seemingly ashamed. Back at home Roxy was tied to a tree for the duration of her visit. However, the next day, Fletcher headed down the driveway and once again ran away from home...this time for good.

For seven years Fletcher had been happy and content living within the boundaries of the Prices' safe haven. He was surrounded by a loving family with every desire right at his paw tips. But Roxy came along and showed him there was more to life than the secure confines of the 30-acre woods and she led her stable companion down the road to disaster. Once he'd tasted the forbidden fruit and sniffed the foreign smells, the pull toward the tempting new world was too strong to resist. In the end, Fletcher lost it all, and he became a scavenger for what had been freely given—a great lesson for all of us.

87

Humbled and Amazed

Let us stop passing judgment on one another.
ROMANS 14:13

You can learn a lot about human nature while watching people on the beach. Teenage girls position themselves to be noticed by muscular young men, dads pass footballs to admiring sons, and little tots squeal in delight at the sudden freedom to play in the sand with no one telling them to stay out of the dirt.

One summer day I was reclining at the beach when I noticed an Asian mother kneeling by her grown son and wiping sand from his feet. Then she humbly slipped his shoes on for him while he casually read a book, never looking at his subservient mother.

Why is that mother waiting on her son hand and foot? I wondered. *Let him wipe his own feet!* I closed my eyes to laze in the sun, and soon the image of this subservient mom drifted away.

Later that evening, cleaned and refreshed from

the day's salt and sand, we crowded into the hotel elevator to search for dinner. Who should be sharing the elevator with us but the family with the feet-wiping mother. We reached the ground floor, and the men parted to let her pass. Then her son awkwardly followed behind. His legs were fitted with metal braces, and his arms were cuffed with stainless steel crutches that swung forward and propelled his lower body toward the door.

The elevator emptied, and the mirrored walls captured my pained expression. Shame filled my heart as I remembered my judgmental attitude. Subservient indeed! Now a whole new list of words describing this mother flooded my mind: loving, tender, caring, pained, sacrificial, and brave.

"Lord, forgive me," I prayed.

You can learn a lot about human nature by watching people on the beach. That day I learned a lot about my own.

88

Lucky to Have a Son like You

Sons are a heritage from the LORD,
children a reward from him.

PSALM 127:3

I don't find amusement parks very amusing. The lines are long, the rides make me queasy, the asphalt is hot, and the food is overpriced. But summer was just about over, and I thought my ten-year-old son might enjoy one last fling. I was feeling quite the martyr as I made this personal sacrifice to take Steven to the park for the day. I hoped he appreciated what a great mom he had.

I wasn't sure he'd come to this realization, so I thought I should bring it to his attention. Just before hurling down the roller-coaster track and into a pool of water, I leaned toward Steven to say, "You are so lucky to have a mom like me to bring you to a place like this." But before the words came out of my mouth, the Holy Spirit stopped me.

Is that what you really want to say? Will those words encourage Steven? Will he feel lucky to have a mom like you?

So I leaned forward, wrapped my arms around my precious young son, and said, "Steven, *I am* so blessed to have a son like you that I can bring to a place like this!"

A dimpled smile spread across his face, and I was thankful for the watery splash of the roller coaster that disguised the tears streaming down my face.

89

The Rose of Sharon

*No eye has seen, no ear has heard, no
mind has conceived, what God has
prepared for those who love him.*

1 CORINTHIANS 2:9

*M*y Bible lay open to the Song of Songs, a
book that some say can be seen as Jesus pursuing His bride, the church. On this day I chose to
read it as if I were reading a love story of Jesus pursuing me as His bride. This became even more real to
me as I read the words in chapter 2, verse 1.

"I am the Rose of Sharon," the woman said to
her beloved.

What is your name? God seemed to ask.

"Lord, my name is Sharon," I whispered aloud.

Look it up, He prompted my heart.

I went to my Bible dictionary and looked up
Sharon. Tears filled my eyes as I discovered that
Sharon was a fertile valley near Mount Carmel.
You see, in my medical chart, somewhere among
the diagnosis and prognosis of years of testing, is

written the word *infertile*. And yet God made sure that my name meant *fertile* before I was even born.

No, I don't have a house full of children with my blood coursing through their veins, but God did make my dream come true. Through the ministry of writing and speaking, I have spiritual children all around the world! When we give our broken dreams to God, He fashions them into a beautiful mosaic that is lovelier than anything we could have ever imagined.

90

Mona Lisa

The king is enthralled by your beauty.
PSALM 45:11

ome say she's one of the most beautiful women in the world, but to me she looked rather ordinary. I stood staring at Leonardo da Vinci's painting of *Mona Lisa* and wondered why it had been revered for so many years. Then the tour guide explained her history. The painting had been moved from King Francis I's castle to Fontainebleau to Paris to Versailles to Napoleon's estate and finally to the Louvre museum in Paris. However, on August 21, 1911, *Mona Lisa* was stolen. The Parisians placed another painting in Mona Lisa's spot, but the citizens missed her terribly. Two years later she emerged in Florence and was returned to Paris. They had their painting back. Today she remains in the Louvre behind bulletproof glass.

Why is she loved today? Because once she was lost, but now she is found. She was stolen from her place of honor, but someone found her, paid the price for her, and put her back in her rightful place. No wonder she's smiling.

So it is with us, dear friend. Once we were lost, but now we've been found and placed back in our rightful place as children of the King. We're not in a museum; our rightful place is in the King's eternal heavenly castle. And that's why we should be smiling too.

91

Boundaries

The boundary lines have fallen for me
in pleasant places;
surely I have a delightful inheritance.

PSALM 16:6

She was at it again. Our eccentric neighbor was in our yard trimming our bushes and pruning our trees. When we built our home, we were blessed with a big backyard 150 feet from our back-door neighbor. The "Smiths" had lived in their home about 14 years before we came along and had land-scaped the back third of our lot as if it were their own. When we bought the property, Mrs. Smith was not happy that we were encroaching on her annex. Over the next several years the boundary line again grew a bit fuzzy for her. Gradually she began inching her way back into our yard, acting as though it were her own.

Finally, after years of pleading, we did what we should have done in the first place. We put up a fence.

This reminds me of what Satan tries to do in our lives. Before we knew Jesus Christ, Satan pretended we were his. He planted thoughts in our minds, sinful acts in our wills, and insecurities in our emotions. But God purchased us at a very high price, and we became His treasured possessions.

Satan knows where the boundary lines around our hearts lie, but just like Mrs. Smith, he creeps back in to plant a little thought here, a little temptation there. The next thing we know, he's standing on a ladder trimming our trees! Well, maybe not our trees, but he's lopping off areas of growth and whacking at anything within his reach.

So what do we do when we see the enemy creeping back on our purchased territory? We show him the title deed signed by God and put up a fence of faith to keep him out! Works every time.

92

Weed Control

Reckless words pierce like a sword,
but the tongue of the wise brings healing.
PROVERBS 12:18

Our yard was a luxurious carpet of luscious green fescue…at least for the first year. But sometime during the second year in our new home, I began to see a few unwelcome visitors in my prize lawn: dandelions, crabgrass, and ground ivy.

"Where did these weeds come from?" I asked Steve.

"They came from seeds that blew in from other places," he said. "Mostly the neighbors' yards."

After the grass came up, all the green blended together nicely, and we hardly noticed the weeds. The following spring, however, we had more weeds and less grass. By the fourth spring we knew if we didn't apply some sort of weed control soon, we would have a yard full of weeds and no grass at all.

Then God reminded me that my yard was a picture of the words we speak in marriage. In the early years we're full of encouraging words and adoring praise. But after a few years, the weeds start to creep in: a sarcastic comment here, a critical jab there, and a nagging spirit in-between. As time passes, if we don't give attention to the verbal weeds, we'll have a marriage with no encouraging words at all.

How do we stop the weeds from spreading? Prayer, the power of the Holy Spirit, and a heart determined to keep our marriages weed free. Eliminating verbal weeds doesn't happen overnight, especially if they've taken root and already done some damage. But with persistent determination, we can eliminate the life-choking weeds and once again sport a beautiful marriage that's the envy of all the homes in the neighborhood.

93

How's Your Reception?

I will listen to what God the LORD will say.
PSALM 85:8

I never wanted a cell phone, but my adolescent son insisted I *needed* one. "You're the only mom I know who doesn't have one," he complained. So for Christmas he purchased a phone with his own ten dollars and convinced my husband to pay the monthly fees.

The first time I tried to use the cellular wonder I discovered I could place a call but I couldn't receive one. When I asked technical support why I was having difficulty, the technician offered several possibilities: I could have been in a dip in the road where the signal could not reach; behind a tall building or wall where the signal was blocked; my antenna was not up; or the battery power was low.

Suddenly I realized the reasons I had trouble receiving calls on my cell phone were the same reasons I sometimes have trouble hearing from God! If my heavenly reception is poor, I need to ask, "Am I in a dip in the road or a depression?" If so, I need to start praising God and get my feet back on level ground. Have I built a tall wall of sin in my life? If so, I need to repent and ask God's forgiveness. Is my spiritual antenna down? If so, I need to tune in with all my senses. Is my spiritual battery running low? If so, I need to pray for a fresh infilling of the Holy Spirit's power in my life.

Apparently, I did need that cell phone after all. God used it to show me how to improve my spiritual reception while traveling down the road of life.

94

Drifting

*We must pay more careful attention, therefore, to
what we have heard, so that we do not drift away.*

HEBREWS 2:1

*L*oran clutched the wheel of the sailing vessel, trying
to hold it steady as the fierce storm threatened
his boat. His heart pounded as his eyes focused on
the two boats in front of him that held his daughters
and other members of his group. Fifteen foot walls
of water tossed the tiny boats like toys in a toddler's
tub. All through the night Loran stood firm, prayed,
and willed the vessels to stay afloat.

In the wee hours of the morning, the wind and
rain came to a halt. The storm had passed, and once
again the boats cut a smooth path across the glassy
sea. Exhausted, the team pulled into a cove to relax,
and Loran jumped into the water, closed his burning
eyes, and floated on his back.

After some time, Loran looked up and noticed
that he had drifted a great distance from the rest of
his party. He swam and swam, fighting the water

with all his might, but the receding tide was too strong for his weary arms. His calls for help went unheard. After what seemed like a lifetime, Loran was still a mile or so from the group.

"O God, don't let me die now!" he prayed.

Miraculously, Loran finally made it back to the boat. As he lay panting on the deck, he realized a great truth. Over the past 24 hours, he'd been in great danger two times—once battling the storm and the other drifting out to sea. But of the two, he was in the most danger when he was drifting carelessly along.

And the same is true in our lives.

95

Seeing the Story

*Open my eyes that I may see
wonderful things in your law.*

PSALM 119:18

I strolled down the aisle of an art museum, quickly glancing at the masterpieces lining the walls. Finally I decided to stop and look carefully at one painting. I don't even remember which one it was. The more I looked, the more I began to see. It was dark on one side and grew lighter on the other. I noticed the expressions on the faces (the longing of a child, the pain of a man), the approaching cloud in the sky, the hues of the clothes, a bare foot, a torn robe, a clenched fist. A story began to unfold before my eyes, and it was as if I were beginning to see into the heart of the artist.

Then I reflected on how I read the Bible at times—like walking briskly through an art gallery and never really stopping to see what the artist intended. I often grab God's Word and read a few verses before running out the door in the morning or closing my eyes at night. And when I do that, I often miss the story.

But God's Word is a masterpiece, and He speaks through every stroke of the writer's pen. Oh, the treasures stored on each page just waiting to be discovered when we slow down enough to really see the story—the masterpiece—as God intended!

96

God's Will

*For God so loved the world that he gave his
one and only Son, that whoever believes in
him shall not perish but have eternal life.*

JOHN 3:16

We have a man down on the play," the announcer
said during the Friday night high school football game in Rose Hill, North Carolina.

LuAnn watched helplessly as her son collapsed
on the field and didn't get up. After a few moments
she rushed from the stands and held Will in her arms
as he took his last breath. A concussion of the heart,
the doctors explained later.

*O God, how can a mother bear the loss of her pre-
cious son?* I prayed.

Then He reminded me of Mary, who watched her
son, battered and bleeding, nailed to a cruel Roman
cross.

"Yes, Lord," I said. "But Jesus came back to life.
Will won't."

I kept my questioning to myself, knowing it wouldn't help anyone.

A few days later LuAnn courageously spoke at her son's funeral. She stood before a crowded congregation and told about Jesus, whom Will loved.

"Accept Jesus as your Savior and receive eternal life," she urged.

Thirty people came to faith that day.

The following week LuAnn spoke at the opponent's school assembly. Again she shared the gospel, and many boys and girls came to Christ.

It was an extraordinary moment when I realized that while Will was not physically raised from the dead, resurrection power took place as hundreds of souls experienced new life in Christ through his story.

Life goes on in Rose Hill. Families still give their children in marriage, celebrate the birth of babies, and play high school football in the fall. And even though Will isn't on the field or in the stands, his memory lives in our hearts and souls.

97

It's What's on the Inside

Man looks at the outward appearance,
but the Lord looks at the heart.

1 Samuel 16:7

The airport was full of hot, weary travelers trying to get home from Mexico. After a three-hour delay in a sweltering concourse, my family finally boarded a rickety plane filled to capacity with disgruntled, sweaty passengers. The air conditioning was on the blink, my tray table was broken, and my son kept insisting he saw duct tape on the left wing. When the flight attendant demonstrated the emergency procedures, we all paid close attention.

When we finally arrived in the U.S., sometime after midnight, my husband's luggage was missing. Since it was an old beat-up suitcase filled with dirty clothes, we weren't too concerned. But the following morning, when Steve couldn't find his Bible, he realized it was in the lost bag.

Suddenly the suitcase was no longer unimportant. This was the Bible I'd given him on our honeymoon, and he had years of notes written on every page. It was one of his most valuable treasures. We had to get the bag back.

Then God spoke to my heart:

> *Isn't it amazing how the realization of what was inside the suitcase changed its value? So it is with My people. Someone might resemble old, beat-up, lost luggage filled with dirty clothes, but I see him as a possible dwelling place for My Son, and that makes him valuable.*

Now when I see someone who has a striking resemblance to that old tattered suitcase, I envision him with a tiny Bible tucked inside, hidden among the clutter, and I begin to see him as my heavenly Father sees him—precious, irreplaceable, and one of His most valuable treasures.

P.S. The airline delivered Steve's suitcase four days later, Bible intact.

98

Who's Talking?

This is my Son, whom I love. Listen to him!
MARK 9:7

ourteen exhausted, sweaty, teenage boys plopped down on the bottom step of the gymnasium bleachers. The basketball coach paced back and forth, lecturing these freshmen on their shortcomings on the court. In the style of a drill sergeant, he yelled, "Who's talking?"

"You are, sir!" the boys shouted back in practiced unison.

Unfortunately for the merry band of athletes, school is not simply a place where sports are played, but it's also an institution for academic advancement. It was time to see just how much advancement had taken place via the dreaded semester exams. During the social studies exam, the room's hushed silence was broken by a faint whisper. The six-foot-five teacher jumped to attention and yelled, "Who's talking?"

Automatically, Chris, one of the basketball players, shot back, "You are, sir!"

The class erupted with laughter. Everyone except the teacher.

"So you want to be smart, do you?" the teacher asked. "Who else in here wants to be smart?"

Over half the class, mostly mischievous boys, raised their hands and snickered. "I want to be smart," they agreed. After-school detention was crowded that week.

It was an innocent mistake—an automatic response—a reflex reaction. But it made Chris a hero for the day among his buddies.

And in a way, he was my hero as well. When my heavenly Teacher speaks to me with that still, small voice, I want to recognize Him. When He asks, "Who's talking?" I pray my response will be just as automatic as Chris's "You are, sir!" I pray I will know His voice and stand at attention to hear what He has to say.

99

The Guestbook

You yourselves are our letter, written on our hearts, known and read by everybody.

2 CORINTHIANS 3:2

Just before leaving our rented condominium at the beach, we peeped into the guestbook and marveled at human nature revealed by its entries. Here are just a few.

- We thoroughly enjoyed our visit. It was our first, but not our last.

- We've decided this is where we want to live. It is a golfer's paradise!

- We enjoyed your villa, but won't be back. Found one a couple doors down for cheaper.

- Hi. I'm Anna. I'm eleven. I'm with my grandma. I love it here and might come back next year!

- It is fabulous here! We played miniature golf, swam, and biked. The ocean is breathtaking. I've never seen it before, so I'm still in awe.

- When we got here, the key wouldn't fit. Almost got run over by a biker. The bed squeaks. Get better service!

Closing the guestbook made me consider what entries I'm writing on the days of my life for all to see. Will I be seen as someone who savored each day with my wonderful family or as a crabby old woman who wanted better service? Will I be seen as someone who enjoyed my time here or preferred life two doors down?

We are only guests in this world. Our true home is heaven, and the legacy we leave behind will be an open book for all to read.

100

Restored

*Create in me a clean heart, O God,
and renew a right spirit within me.*
PSALM 51:10 (ESV)

I lay flat on my back, gazing at one of the most incredible paintings in the world—the ceiling of the Sistine Chapel. From 1508 to 1512, Michelangelo lay on his back and painstakingly painted one gigantic historical, biblical account of man. But almost as soon as the paintings were completed, they began to fade. Years of fading, ill attempts to cover the paintings with varnish, and layers of smoke and dirt made the original masterpiece barely visible.

In 1981 a special cleaning solution called AB-57 was discovered. After eight years of gingerly cleaning the masterpiece inch by inch, the beauty, the colors, and the intricate details of the paintings were brought back to life. For the first time in nearly 500 years, spectators saw the masterpiece the way the artist intended.

But not everyone was pleased with the restoration.

Some local folk rebelled at the newly restored work of art. They had become accustomed to the dulling grime left by years of pollution and cried, "We want our paintings back!"

It was difficult for me to fathom anyone not appreciating the vivid colors that the original artist intended. Then God reminded me of His desire to restore fallen humanity. Some people are much more comfortable with the years of filth and grime that mar God's original works of art, and they rebel at the idea of restoration. But God's desire is to cleanse us and restore us to the beautiful work of His original design.

When we yield our life's canvas to God, He fills our days with vibrant colors, breathtaking hues, and magnificent marvels—what the Artist intended all along.

101

I Have Called You by Name

Fear not, for I have redeemed you;
I have called you by name, you are mine.
ISAIAH 43:1 (ESV)

A few years after I was married, I noticed my dad becoming forgetful. At first it was small idiosyncrasies: forgetting an order at work, misplacing his keys, not remembering what day it was, drawing a blank on a close friend's name. Then it progressed to more serious absentminded behavior: forgetting where he parked, coming home to take my mom to the market when he'd taken her an hour before, becoming confused when taking measurements for cabinets—something he'd been doing for more than 30 years. In 1987 our greatest fears were confirmed. Dad had Alzheimer's disease. He was 56 years old.

For ten years I watched a strapping, quick-witted entrepreneur reduced to a man who couldn't remember how to speak, button his shirt, or move a spoon from his plate to his mouth. But my most heart-wrenching day was the day he forgot my name.

As I lamented this great loss, God assured me that He, my heavenly Father, would never forget my name. It's engraved on the palm of His hand.

And now that my dad has gone to heaven, God reminded me that the two of them speak of me often, and never once had Dad forgotten my name.

102

Race to Victory

*I have fought the good fight, I have finished
the race, I have kept the faith.*

2 TIMOTHY 4:7

*I*t's a bird! It's a plane! No, it's Steven's shoe!"

My son was in the second lap of the 1600-meter race when his shoe flew into the air. Fans laughed and pointed at the runner with his sock flapping like a worn sole. Would he stop? Would he slow down? Would his sock stay on?

With teammates cheering him on, Steven amazingly sped up. He could feel the eyes of the crowd pressing in on him as his sock began inching its way down his ankle. Undaunted, he continued on. The focus of the race changed as fans became more interested in what Steven would do than who would win. When he crossed the finish line first, the crowd erupted in applause and laughter. He had recorded his best personal time while overcoming unexpected adversity.

"I knew everybody was looking at me," Steven

said later. "It wasn't just a race anymore. They were watching to see what I'd do. It made me go faster. It made me want to do better."

It was an extraordinary race for Steven and an extraordinary moment with God for me. He showed me how closely others watch us run the great race of life when we're faced with unexpected difficulties.

"Will she buckle? Will she quit? Will she turn back?" spectators ask.

But when we press on, despite the struggles of life, despite the laughter of the crowd, we'll hear the applause of heaven cheering us on to victory. And onlookers will be amazed at the courageous persistence that only God can give.

103

Lassoing Contest

*We take captive every thought to
make it obedient to Christ.*

2 CORINTHIANS 10:5

We all sat on the edge of our seats as the cowboy waited, poised in his saddle, anticipating the calf's release from the chute. It was my first rodeo, but I knew what to expect. The corral door swung open, and the calf burst out of the gate. The cowboy on horseback raced after the bucking, twisting, galloping animal, lassoed its neck, and threw it to the ground. He quickly wrapped the rope around the calf's legs, tied them securely in place, and raised his arms in victory.

The clock continued to run for a few seconds as the scorekeeper waited to make sure the calf was indeed a captive. Then the cowboy's time was displayed on the scoreboard. Time and time again cowhands lassoed little calves, secured them in place, and listened to the applause of the crowd.

I was feeling a bit sorry for the calves even though

they were released as soon as the time was logged. But the Lord prodded my mind to note that I was watching an example of how to "take every thought captive."

You see, sometimes wild, unruly thoughts burst through the door of our minds: negative, rebellious, fearful, angry, worrisome, jealous thoughts. When that happens, our reaction should be like a cowboy's. As soon as an ungodly thought bursts through the gate, we need to ride up hot on that thought's heels, lasso it with God's truth, throw it back into the dust where it came from, and tie it up with faith.

The quicker we do it the better, and if we listen closely, we'll hear the applause of heaven with each victory.

104

The Right Credentials

*In him and through faith in him we may
approach God with freedom and confidence.*

EPHESIANS 3:12

*Y*ou're not supposed to be here. Where's your backstage pass? You're in a lot of trouble!"

I stood frozen in the elevator with a disgruntled, accusing security guard pointing his finger in my face. He pulled out his walkie-talkie and was not afraid to use it.

Justin Clairmont and I were on our way backstage to visit with his mother, Patsy, at a Women of Faith conference. I didn't have a pass, but Justin assured me he could get me through. Just as I was about to explain this to the security guard, Justin stepped forward and showed his credentials.

"Excuse me, sir," he said. "I'm the son of one of the speakers. I have a pass and she's with me."

"That's right, mister," I added with a sudden show of courage. "He's Patsy Clairmont's son, and I'm with him."

"Oh, okay then," the guard said as he hopped off the elevator to find other dangerous Christian women attending the conference.

The conference was wonderfully encouraging, but my most extraordinary moment was on the elevator.

One day I will leave this earth to make my way through heaven's doors. I imagine Satan, the accuser, will be lurking in the shadows, waiting to call me unworthy and questioning my credentials. "You don't belong here!" he will say. "Where's your pass? What are your credentials"

Then, just as Patsy's son stepped forward, Jesus Christ, God's Son, will step forward and say, "Leave her alone! She's with me. I'm all the credentials she needs."

105

Playing with the Pros

We all, like sheep, have gone astray.

ISAIAH 53:6

One vacation we rented a condominium that overlooked the eighth fairway of a pristine golf course. My son, Steven, and I watched as golfers dressed to the nines took their strokes.

Ping went the ball against the clubhead. *Splash* went the sound of the hooked ball landing in the creek by our deck. *Ping* went another ball. *Bonk* went the sound of the sliced ball bounding off a rooftop. Steven and I stifled laughs as we watched 40 "expert" golfers slice and hook balls to the left and right of the fairway. Occasionally a golfer hit a ball straight and long with perfect form and trajectory.

"Steven," I said, "what you're seeing today is life being played out before your very eyes. Some people look good, have the right clothes, buy the best toys, and even know the right lingo. But that doesn't make them pros. We all slice, hook, and get off course at times. It's the rare person who drives it straight down the middle and stays on the fairway throughout the entire course, and that only comes with practice and God's grace. Many golfers go to classes, but they refuse to change their harmful habits and repeat the same mistakes time and time again."

"What I don't get," Steven said, "is why these guys keep on playing. They look so frustrated."

"I think it's because occasionally they hit a good shot, and it gives them hope," I said.

About the time Steven and I finished watching this amusing display, my husband walked in and tossed his clubs on the floor.

"How'd you play today?" I asked.

"Don't ask. But I did hit a couple of good shots."

Steven and I looked at each other and laughed.

106

Just a Bit Off

Make a joyful noise to the LORD, all the earth!
PSALM 100:1 (ESV)

I love to hear the familiar sound of our church bells ringing the hour in the distance. There's something about it that reminds me that God is near and time is in His hands. Occasionally the bells play a familiar hymn for the entire community to enjoy. Well, at least that's the plan. But the truth is, the bells are just a bit off-key, and if the sound weren't coming from a church steeple, the neighbors would probably call in a noise complaint.

As I winced at the church bells' rendition of "Amazing Grace," God reminded me that most of the people that fill churches each week are…well, a little bit off-key too.

I remember the pastor who married Steve and me and his tendency to make up words by combining them. (For example, creation and reality became creality.) Then there was the friend who preached his first sermon to a large traditional congregation and pierced the silence with his pastoral prayer by booming, "Almighty Gog." And the elderly pastor who asked my friend to repeat her wedding vows, "Do you, Ellen, take this man to be your lawfully wedded husband in sickness and in death."

But it's not just leaders who blunder. We're all a bunch of mere humans who need God's amazing grace.

Come to think about it, the off-key church bells seem very appropriate. God puts the song in our hearts, and while we sing with all our might, sometimes it comes out just a bit off-key. But it's still music to His ears.

107

Running with the Pack

Run in such a way that you may win.
1 Corinthians 9:24 (NASB)

The boys had never won a race, and they didn't believe they could. When Coach Down met with my son's cross-country team for the first time, he'd never seen such a bunch of defeated, lackadaisical boys in all his life. But he took on the challenge of sparking a tiny ray of hope.

"Guys, have you ever noticed on TV how wolves run? They run in a pack—all together to capture their prey. That's what I want you to do. Races are won by the accumulated points of the entire team. If our runners in the back are faster than their runners in the back, we can win this race. We're going to learn how to run with the pack."

Coach Down could hardly believe his eyes when he saw "the pack" emerge from the woods at the next cross-country race. The boys took third place and whooped and hollered because for the first time they hadn't come in last. It was a watershed moment as they realized they did indeed have a chance at victory.

Before the last race of the season, Coach Down encouraged each runner to trim ten seconds off his previous time, and they each agreed they could. In the end, it wasn't the runner who took first place, or even second, that determined the winning team. It was the accumulated points of the boys running with the pack that took the team to victory and a first-place championship.

As I watched the boys celebrate with tears in my eyes, God reminded me what working as a team can accomplish—whether we're running in a footrace or the great race of life.

108

Your Scars Are Beautiful to God

Let the redeemed of the LORD tell their story.
PSALM 107:2 (TNIV)

It was just a few days after Easter, and I was reading about the resurrection of Jesus in the Gospel of John, chapter 20. I had read the story many times before, but this time God revealed something I'd never noticed before.

In my mind's eye I saw Mary weeping in the predawn mist hovering over the garden and the tomb where Jesus' body had been laid three days earlier. I saw her running to tell the disciples of her conversation with the risen Lord. I imagined Peter and John gazing into the empty tomb.

"He's not here," John whispered as he peered inside. "His body is gone."

And later, as the disillusioned band of disciples huddled in their hiding place, I saw Jesus appear in their midst. He didn't knock. He didn't open the door. He simply appeared.

"Peace be with you," Jesus said.

Then I realized that the disciples didn't recognize Him. He looked like Jesus, talked like Jesus, but... how could He be Jesus?

In order to convince them, Jesus made a simple gesture. He held out His arms and revealed His nail-pierced hands. He lifted up His tunic and uncovered His spear-pierced side.

It was then that they believed.

O God, I prayed, *they didn't recognize Jesus until He showed them His scars.*

Yes, My child, He seemed to say. *This is what I wanted you to see. They didn't recognize Jesus until He showed them His scars, and this is how others still recognize Him today—when men and women who have experienced the healing of past wounds are not ashamed to show their scars to a hurting world.*

109

UPS Yes!

*I am the vine; you are the branches. If you
remain in me and I in you, you will bear much
fruit; apart from me you can do nothing.*

JOHN 15:5 (TNIV)

As I walked past my neighbor's house I noticed
that this was a UPS pick-up day. Susan has a
booming home business creating primitive folk art
originals. When she has a shipment ready for pick-up,
she puts a sign by her mailbox that reads "UPS Yes."
The delivery man sees the sign and knows he needs
to stop. On other days she puts out a sign that reads
"UPS No," and he knows his services aren't needed.

Day after day I watched the alternating signs by
Susan's mailbox until one day God got my attention.
Is that what you do with Me?

I realized that sometimes I treat God like Susan's
UPS man. On days when my burdens are heavy, my
to-do list is overwhelming, and my patience is running thin, I cry out, "God, help me today!" But on
days when life is clicking right along and I think I

have everything under control, I have the attitude, "Don't need You today, Lord. Thanks anyway."

In reality, every day is a "God help me" day. Apart from His help and intervention, I can do nothing. Oh, I can be busy, but I will not be productive or, as Jesus said, "fruitful." I love the old hymn by Annie S. Hawks that says,

> I need Thee, O I need Thee,
> Every hour I need Thee;
> O bless me now, my Savior,
> I come to Thee.

What does the sign over your heart say today?

110

A Not-So-Quiet Quiet Time

He put a new song in my mouth,
a hymn of praise to our God.

PSALM 40:3

*C*ould you please be quiet and leave me alone!" I commanded the squawking bird. "You are completely ruining my quiet time with God!" As soon as I sat down on my patio to do my morning devotion, a little finch darted from a flower basket that had become its summer home. He perched on a tree in front of me angrily squawking in my direction. After several minutes of constant badgering, I decided to give that bird a piece of my mind.

"Look, buddy," I said, "who planted those flower baskets in the first place? I did! Who hung and fertilized them? I did! And who waters them daily? I do! Don't you come out here complaining to me because I chose to sit here and enjoy what I've planted. They're mine in the first place, and I'm just letting you live there. And you should be thankful for that. Beside, you're making a terrible mess!"

He continued hurling insults my way, and after a while I realized his angry complaints had a familiar ring to them. In fact, they sounded a lot like my own. Oh, how I complain when situations don't go my way, when someone messes up my plans, or when someone invades my space. My, my, my.

Then God spoke to my heart. *Who made this earth in the first place? Who planted and watered all you have before you? This whole earth and all it contains is Mine. I'm just letting you live here. And besides, sometimes you make a terrible mess. Stop your squawking and start chirping the song I've put in your heart.*

It was a not-so-quiet time, but God's message came through loud and clear.

111

Go, Stu!

Encourage one another.

1 THESSALONIANS 5:11

The boys lined up on the starting mark. The starter's pistol fired and 70 cross-country runners left in a cloud of dust and cheers. My nephew, Stu, was among the herd. As soon as he took off, his mother, Pat, picked up her 36-inch megaphone and began to yell, "Go, Stu!"

The boys disappeared down the 3.1-mile trail in the woods, but that didn't deter Pat's enthusiasm. "Go, Stu!" she continued to yell as she ran to strategic spots along the trail where the boys would pass by. My embarrassed husband stood a safe distance away, pretending he didn't know who we were. Pat had no shame.

"Pat, do you think he can hear you when he's deep in the woods?"

"I don't know, but if there's a chance he can, I want him to hear my voice cheering for him," she said.

For 16 minutes this dynamo continued to pump confidence and courage into her son's heart.

Later I asked, "Stu, when you're running in the woods, can you hear your mother cheering for you?"

"Oh yes," he said. "I can hear her the whole way."

"And what does that do for you?" I asked.

"It makes me not want to quit. When my legs and lungs ache, when I feel like I'm going to get sick, I hear my mom cheering for me, and it makes me not want to stop."

What a beautiful picture of the encouragement we can give each other in the great race of life. An encouraging word, offered at just the right moment, could mean the difference between someone finishing well, or collapsing along the way.

112

The Hidden Treasure

*He who did not spare his own Son, but
gave him up for us all—how will he not
also...graciously give us all things?*

ROMANS 8:32

I stood at Steven's bedroom door, watching this now 17-year-old son sleep in a tangle of sheets and limbs. He was six-feet tall, needed a shave, and sported a mass of shaggy brown hair.

Lord, I prayed, *You know how much I love children and how I always longed to be a mom. I know Your ways are higher than our ways, and that You are my heavenly Father who knows what's best for me. But, God, would You show me a purpose behind the pain of infertility and the loss of a child? Why was there just one?*

Then God's Word washed over me: "For God so loved the world that he gave his one and only Son, that whoever believes in him shall not perish but have eternal life."

"Is that You, Lord?" I asked.

"For God so loved the world that he gave his one and only Son, that whoever believes in him shall not perish but have eternal life."

The words washed over me again like a spring rain on parched ground. For the first time in my life I truly grasped the height, the depth, and the breadth of those familiar words from John 3:16.

You see, I have a one and only son. I love many people in this world, but none enough to sacrifice my only son. And yet God loved us that much. He loved you and me enough to sacrifice His one and only Son in order to give us eternal life.

With tears spilling down my cheeks, I thanked God for helping me understand His great love—for giving me a living, breathing picture indelibly impressed on my mind and in my heart. If that was the only purpose behind the years of infertility and loss of a child, that was enough.

113

Resting in the Palm

She watches over the affairs of her household.
PROVERBS 31:27

From the second-story porch of our beach cottage I discovered a turtledove nestled in the branches of a palm tree. Clustered under her downy wings were three tiny eggs. All during the week, when strong winds blew sheets of pelting rain, when children ran up and down the steps by her nest, when other birds flaunted their feathered freedom, the mother bird remained undaunted in her task.

On the last day of our vacation I joined Mrs. Turtledove for one last cup of coffee before the others in the house began to stir.

Lord, I prayed (for God was sitting on the porch with us), *I believe you put this momma bird here for a reason. What did you want me to learn?*

Just as I lifted my eyes, the dove rose from her nest to reveal three tiny hatchlings. Then I knew. God was showing me a picture of a contented mother doing what He had fashioned her to do during this period of her life. Regardless of the storms, regardless of what other birds were doing around her, regardless of the endless stream of activity, she was steadfast in her calling.

You do what I've called you to do. Rest in the palm of My hand, and all too soon, your *young charge will fly away and leave the nest behind.*

About that time, my six-foot teenage son sleepily stumbled out onto the porch. I'm not sure if he saw the tears in my eyes as I looked at his ruffled hair, sleepy eyes, and a face that needed a shave.

"Hey, bud, look," I said. "The eggs hatched today."

114

Old Faithful

Above all else, guard your heart,
for it is the wellspring of life.
PROVERBS 4:23

There she blows!" we all shouted as Old Faithful shot into the air. "Right on time."

We had traveled to Yellowstone National Park and waited for over an hour to see Old Faithful shoot some 8400 gallons of boiling water 150 feet into the air. The geyser show lasted about 3 minutes and held a repeat performance every 76 minutes or so. The seemingly endless supply of water below the surface of the earth, combined with heat and pressure, have provided a watery display that has fascinated tourists for years.

Just a few miles away we made a quick stop to observe sulfur-filled ponds that bubbled up from the earth. These putrid smelling puddles may have been another world wonder, but we didn't see many tourists hanging around to gaze at their beauty. It was a click of the camera and then an escape from the area as quickly as possible. The stench was unbearable.

As we drove away from the park, I reflected on how the two world wonders resembled the conditions of the human heart. The heart can be a magnificent display of faithful beauty and splendor that makes people want to gaze in wonder. Or it can be a repugnant puddle of putrid disgust that causes them to run the other way. With all the pollutants in our world today, it's easy for a heart to become contaminated. To keep a heart pure requires an endless supply of pure, living water that runs deep below the surface.

With God's never-ending supply, we too can be a world wonder—an Old Faithful—that people love to see.

115

Gone with the Wind

*When Moses was forty years old, he decided to visit
his fellow Israelites...After forty years [more] had
passed, an angel appeared to Moses in the flames of
a burning bush in the desert near Mount Sinai.*

ACTS 7:23,30

*I*t was the rerelease of *Gone with the Wind*. Steven
had never seen the epic drama, so we grabbed our
popcorn and settled down to enjoy a bit of history.
We watched as the plantation owners of the Old
South held grand parties and Scarlett O'Hara batted
her eyelashes at all the men crowded around her.
The scenery changed as the Civil War began, and
the Old South began to crumble. Scarlett became
a widow (twice), and Rhett Butler tried to save the
day.

After about two hours, Miss Scarlett stood on a
hillside with Atlanta burning in the background and
shook her fist in the air. "As God is my witness, I will
never be hungry again," she declared.

Then the curtain fell.

Steven looked at me and said, "That was a strange way to end."

I pointed his attention back to the screen, which read: *Intermission*.

Have you ever felt like Scarlett? Your plans go up in flames, your friends desert you, and you long for the good life? I think the producers had a good idea. Maybe *we* need to take an intermission—take a deep breath, refocus on God, and remember that He's not finished with the grand drama of our lives yet.

Perhaps we're just in an intermission.

116

Paul's Return...or Not

We eagerly await a Savior from [heaven], the Lord Jesus Christ, who, by the power that enables him to bring everything under his control, will transform our lowly bodies so that they will be like his glorious body.

PHILIPPIANS 3:20-21

luffy, you were a naughty boy when you ran out in the street on Monday." The woman in front of me at the veterinarian's office scolded her cat as though it were a wayward child. She cocked her head as if listening and continued, "Oh, was it Tuesday?"

Those of us standing within earshot of this duo felt a bit uncomfortable at the one-sided conversation. Then she turned to us and explained.

"Fluffy is the reincarnation of a deceased friend of mine. My good friend, Paul, passed away not too long ago. Then two days later, Fluffy appeared on my doorstep out of nowhere, and he has been with me ever since."

Then this woman encouraged us fellow pet owners to join in the conversation with her feline. I decided that my dog didn't really need to see the doctor that day after all and eased my way to the door.

Driving home, God assured me that He had plans for my afterlife, and it didn't involve being reincarnated as a cat, a cow, or any other furry beast. I was going to have a heavenly body that resembled Jesus Christ's—imperishable, incorruptible, and clothed in glory and honor.

And God knew exactly where Paul was...and he wasn't at the veterinarian's office.

117

Calming the Storm

*He got up and rebuked the wind and the raging
waters; the storm subsided, and all was calm.*

LUKE 8:24

Held captive in the grocery store by a fierce thunderstorm, I heard a child's cry—not an unusual sound in a grocery store. But something about the cry gave me pause. Was it a sleepy cry? Was it hunger? I couldn't tell.

She stood just two feet tall, this crying urchin, reaching for her mom to pick her up. "Shut up!" the weary mother barked. Then the crying toddler wandered around the counter to the cashier and held up her tiny arms. The uncomfortable young girl ignored the toddler's plea and refused to make eye contact. Then she looked at me, this child starving for attention.

We locked eyes, and she took this as an invitation. It was. She waddled over, wrapped her arms around my legs, and calmly placed her thumb in her mouth as she rested her drenched face on my skin. After a moment or so, she leaned back and reached up with hopeful arms.

"May I pick her up?" I asked her mom.

When I received an affirmative nod, I embraced the tear-soaked child as she nestled her wet cheek against my chest. Automatically I rocked back and forth.

Yes, it was hunger after all.

All too soon the storm cloud passed and the pelting rain slowed to a drizzle. Reluctantly I handed the toddler back to her mother, who most likely was hungry for love as well.

As I walked to the parking lot, I was now the one with tears streaming down my cheeks as I realized Jesus still calms the storms—and sometimes He uses our arms to do it.

118

Something to Smile About

I praise you because I am fearfully
and wonderfully made.

PSALM 139:14

It was a tense drive to school on a crisp December morning. Just a few months before, Steven had transferred to a large high school, and while his social life was thriving, his grades were on the decline.

I was tired. He was frustrated. I was disappointed. He was sullen.

We had previously met with the chemistry and English teachers, and today it was Mrs. Morris in Spanish 3. After the conference, I got into my car to leave. A security guard blew his whistle and held up his hand for me to stop.

What now? I grumbled.

A bus filled with handicapped teens began unloading in front of me, blocking my path. All I could do was wait...and watch.

That's when I saw him. He was about 15 years old, I guess. He wore thick glasses and a tattered jacket.

His limbs twitched as he tried to propel his frail body forward, clinging to the doors of the bus to steady his steps. Three sunny adults waited to welcome him to another day of life. One woman held his arms to guide him down the steps. Another placed a helmet on his head, and a third held a walker steady until he could grasp the cold, steel handles. Then he grinned at the threesome, proud of his accomplishment.

I drove out of the parking lot with tears streaming down my cheeks, forgetting why I had been so upset with Steven.

"How was the teacher conference?" my husband asked when he came home from work.

"Oh, it was fine. But let me tell you about the conference I had with God in the parking lot."

119

The King's Kids

I will sing to the LORD,
for he has been good to me.
PSALM 13:6

The angels were hovering low in our church on this particular Sunday morning. It was a special day for a group of ten "kids" known as the "King's Kids." They were leading worship by singing a special song—only many of them couldn't carry a tune, walk on their own, or even control their limbs.

We sat in silence as the unlikely band of worship leaders stumbled onto the stage. Each of these children of God had a disability and visible handicap. They lined up on the stage, many with adults standing behind them to support them, physically and emotionally. Kristen, a young lady with Down syndrome, appeared to be the leader. She stood out in front of the others with confidence, strength, and passion.

The sound track began, and the King's Kids began to "sing" with their hands in sign language. "Press on," their hands proclaimed. With wide sweeping motions and uninhibited praise, Kristen sang with arms and hands to the One who loved her most.

One girl in particular caught my eye. She was not able to do the signs by herself. Her limbs were much too weak and uncontrolled. I watched as she leaned into a woman standing behind her and surrendered her arms and hands, and the woman moved her hands in tandem with the others.

That is what I want you to do, God seemed to say. *Lean into Me, relinquish control, and allow Me to move your life in a symphony of worship.*

The King's Kids had no words, but God's love echoed through their lives. Which is exactly what God wants to do through us.

120

Mixed Messages

Out of the same mouth come praise and cursing.
My brothers, this should not be.

JAMES 3:10

Catherine and I set out for a lazy summer stroll around the neighborhood just before dusk. When we arrived back at her house, she invited me in, and before I knew it, it was almost ten o'clock.

I called my husband, sure that he would be worried. When he didn't answer the phone, I left the following message: "Steve, I was calling to let you know I'm at Catherine's. I thought you'd be worried, but apparently you don't even care because you won't pick up the phone!" *Click.* I said my goodbyes and left feeling somewhat dejected. But who should I meet along the way? My worried husband riding his bike frantically through the neighborhood searching for me. When we got back home, I quickly erased the phone message.

A few weeks later Steve called me from work.

"Sharon, have you listened to the answering machine lately?"

"No, why?"

"Well, I think there's something on there you need to hear."

I used my cell phone to call our home phone, and this is what I heard: "Hello (the voice of a sweet Southern belle), you've reached the Jaynes' residence. We're unable to answer the phone right now—(Enter the voice of Cruella De Vil)—I was calling to let you know I'm at Catherine's. I thought you'd be worried, but apparently you don't even care because you won't pick up the phone! (Return of sweet Southern belle.) At the sound of the beep, leave your number, and we'll get back with you as soon as possible." *Beep.*

The phone company explained that a lightning strike had jumbled the message.

Lord, this is so embarrassing, I prayed.

Yes, it is, He said.

Okay, Lord, I got the message.

Unfortunately, so did a lot of other people.

Gift by the Sea

For the message of the cross is foolishness
to those who are perishing, but to us who
are being saved it is the power of God.

1 CORINTHIANS 1:18

The sea breeze blew the tangles from my knotted nerves, and a choir of songbirds announced the dawn of a new day. Myrtle bushes bursting with fuchsia blossoms added splashes of color to the sandy landscape. Jumping fish performed acrobatic feats for an audience of one.

The beach is my favorite place on earth. On this spring morning I rose to have a cup of coffee with God before the others in the cottage stirred from their slumber. I relaxed in a rocking chair on the porch, surrounded by coastal beauty, and watched the lazy water in a canal meander by.

God urged me to look at a reflection in the water, and I saw a simple wooden cross. Upon closer inspection, I realized this was actually a reflection of an old forgotten clothesline post, but to me it was much more. This cross was God's reminder that in all the majesty of His creation, the cross of two wooden beams remains the most beautiful of all. Two simple beams displayed to the entire world the surpassing greatness of His love, the invaluable richness of His grace, and the unfathomable depth of His mercy to all who believe.

And that is more beautiful than any blooming flower, more melodious than the song of any feathered friend, and more powerful than the surf on any shore.

122

The Call

I love you, O LORD, my strength.
PSALM 18:1

It was a surprising phone call.

Steven was a sophomore in college, and he didn't call home as often as this mother's heart would have liked. But I was trying my best to let him go and grow. We had given him roots, and now it was time to give him wings. So I was delighted when I noticed his number on my caller ID.

We chatted about his classes and what he was learning. He caught me up on his roommate and various other students from our hometown. Then he asked me what I'd been up to, how the ministry was going, and what I'd been working on.

We got ready to say goodbye, and I said, "Wait a minute. Don't you want anything?"

"Nope," he answered. "I just called to talk."

After we said our "goodbyes" and "I love yous," I sat reveling in Steven's call. He didn't call because he needed money for books, had a question about car insurance, or wanted help with rent. He just called to talk...because he loved me.

I wondered, *Is this how God feels when we talk to Him, not because we need something or we're in a bind, but because we love Him?*

In this extraordinary moment I decided to call on my heavenly Father more often through prayer...not because I want something, but just to say how much I love Him.

123

Mirage

Godliness with contentment is great gain.
1 TIMOTHY 6:6

lutter. Flutter. *Bang!* Flutter. Flutter. *Bang!*
Momma and Papa Bluebird danced in front of our
sunroom windows, trying frantically to break
through the glass. Time and time again they torpedoed their feathered heads against the panes.

What were they pursuing? What caught their eye?
Why were they so persistent? After three days of this
featherbrained banging, I decided to look at the situation from their perspective. I stepped out onto the
patio, stood in front of the windows, and there it
was. In the reflection of the glass was their birdhouse,
some 30 feet behind me.

Mr. and Mrs. Bluebird's lovely cedar-shingled
home with a decorative finial sat on a tall pole
nestled under the protective branches of an old oak
tree. Their bed and breakfast came equipped with an
adjoining spa—a concrete birdbath surrounded by

fragrant rosebushes bursting with red blossoms and by a carpet of white impatiens.

But instead of being satisfied with their high-rise estate, they were banging their heads against the pane, striving for a mirage, a mere reflection.

Suddenly I saw my own reflection in the birds' senseless activity. Sometimes I flutter about striving to get what I already have. God has given us incredible spiritual riches, and all the window dressings of this world are merely mirages of happiness.

I wondered, *Why would we ever desire a mere reflection when God offers the real thing?*

124

A Healthy Dose of Perspective

This is the day the LORD has made;
let us rejoice and be glad in it.
PSALM 118:24

It was just a quick checkup at the doctor's office… or at least that's what it was supposed to be. My to-do list resembled a mile-long scroll, and several deadlines loomed like a thundercloud ready to burst. But I knew the appointment would take just a few minutes, just enough time to catch my breath.

I checked in with the receptionist, grabbed a few outdated magazines, and waited. And waited. And waited. After 35 minutes a nurse finally took me back to an examination room, where I waited and waited and waited. By the time the doctor came in the room, I was pretty upset. My time was important too, you know.

"Sharon, I'm sorry I'm late," he began. "I had to

tell a patient she has terminal cancer and, well, it took longer than I thought it would."

Tears pooled in my eyes, and my icy countenance melted into a puddle on the shiny tile floor. I was upset about not checking frivolous errands off my to-do list, and the woman in the next room was pondering how she was going to spend her last days on earth.

Yes, I did have a checkup that day. God examined my heart to see that my perspective on life needed surgery. What's really important? My silly list of errands? No. What should be at the top of my to-do list today and every day is to celebrate each day as an incredible gift from God.

125

Jump In

*I trust in God's unfailing love
for ever and ever.*

PSALM 52:8

I was sitting on the balcony of a condominium at the beach listening to the excited squeals and splashes as children played in the pool. One little girl caught my attention. She appeared to be about six years old and wore bright yellow water wings wrapped around her arms like blood pressure cuffs. She stood on the side of the pool nervously flapping her arms, as her daddy stood poised in waist deep water with his arms outstretched.

"Come on, honey, you can do it," he said. "Go ahead and jump. I'm right here."

"But I'm scared," she whined and flapped.

"Don't be afraid. I'm right here."

The bantering continued, and I marveled at the father's patience. Finally, after fifteen minutes of coaxing, she jumped! Applause and laughter erupted from observers around the pool and on the surrounding balconies. By the end of the morning the little girl was confidently making her way across the once seemingly treacherous waters.

Then I had an extraordinary moment with God as I realized that sometimes I am that little girl standing on the side of the pool.

"Come on, you can do it" my heavenly Father calls. "Go ahead and jump. I'm right here."

"But I'm scared," I say.

"Don't be afraid, My child. I'm right here. I'm not going to let anything happen to you."

So I've learned to jump in with both feet...and never let go of His hand.

126

God's Post-it Notes

*Since the creation of the world God's
invisible qualities—his eternal power and
divine nature—have been clearly seen, being
understood from what has been made.*

ROMANS 1:20

I believe one of the greatest inventions of the twentieth century was the Post-it Note. First there was yellow. Then came fuchsia, turquoise, buttercup, and magenta. From full-page mega notes to tiny little strips, sticky notes have saved me from embarrassment, kept me organized, and helped me memorize. Mostly they have served as visual reminders of information, events, and appointments not to forget.

But visual reminders of things not to forget didn't begin with Post-it Notes. They began with God. All through life God places Post-it Notes on our days to remind us of Him. Just today I jotted down a few Post-its God placed throughout my day.

- The sunrise with swirls of mist rising from the lake behind my home

- A vibrant red male cardinal and his demure wife sharing the birdfeeder
- Boisterous Canadian geese flying in V-formation across the sky
- Tulip bulbs peeping through the ground
- The weeping willow praising God in the breeze
- A monarch butterfly perched on the windowsill
- Midday sunlight dancing on the water
- Orange, magenta, and red streaks across the sky as the sun bid goodnight
- A sliver of white in the inky sky with a smattering of twinkles all around
- My husband's hand reaching for me in the night

Each and every one of these sightings were God's reminders to me that He has infused my life with His presence. Through His creation, God longs for us to see and discover, observe and remember His creative beauty, His enduring grace, and His fathomless love.

127

Hand in Hand

*Two are better than one, because they have
a good return for their work: If one falls
down, his friend can help him up.*

ECCLESIASTES 4:9-10

Looking out my den window I noticed two of my neighbors puttering slowly down the street. Ernestine, with her bald head snuggled in a woolen cap, held tightly to Patti's supporting arm. Patti's chestnut hair, just two inches long, shone like a victor's crown—the crown of a cancer survivor.

In May 1998, Patti felt a lump, and a doctor's visit confirmed she had cancer. For three months she endured chemotherapy followed by seven weeks of radiation, five days a week. As God would have it, her final treatment fell on Thanksgiving Day. Yes, she had much to be thankful for—a full life, a loving husband, and Ernestine.

During Patti's cancer treatment, Ernestine was right by her side, an extension of Jesus' hands and feet, providing love, encouragement, and support.

One year after her final radiation treatment, Patti was given the opportunity to return the kindness to Ernestine.

In November 1999, a trip to the doctor revealed that Ernestine had lymphoma. Now Patti was the nurturer. She took Ernestine to her first chemotherapy and explained what to expect. She told Ernestine what to eat, where to go to have a wig made, and how to deal with depression.

As I watched the twosome make their way down the street that chilly November day, I whispered a prayer, thanking God for girlfriends in God—friends with whom we can be His hands and feet when one is too weak to walk unassisted, His strong arm when a burden is too heavy to bear alone, and His voice when a friend has forgotten the words to the song in her heart.

128

Laughing in the Face of Fear

So do not fear, for I am with you;
do not be dismayed, for I am your God.
ISAIAH 41:10

Twenty tourists piled into a small boat to mean-der down the lazy river in the fantasy world of Universal Studios. We were in the make-believe town of Amity, where the man-eating shark, Jaws, made us all afraid to go into the ocean back in the late 70s.

We slowly drifted along when suddenly the waters began to stir. Oh no! Just as we suspected, a giant shark attacked our boat! Women screamed, babies cried, and one overall-clad, hefty man in the back burst out laughing. Soon his contagious laughter caused an avalanche of giggles throughout the boat. Each of the four times during the ride that Jaws appeared and lunged at our boat, the laughing man had the same effect—side-splitting, rip-roaring laughter.

I'm not sure the tour guide had ever seen any-thing like it.

The man knew the shark was fake. To him the attack was...well, funny. Suddenly God showed me how to face the fears that attack my life. Most of the time what I worry about is not even real—it's some-thing I've conjured up. When I know the truth of Scripture and that God is in total control of my life, I have nothing to fear. Upon closer inspection, many of my fears are simply something to laugh about.

Jaws? I'm not worried. He's just a big fake.

129

It's Not Over 'til It's Over

Thanks be to God! He gives us the victory
through our Lord Jesus Christ.

1 CORINTHIANS 15:57

*I*t's called "March Madness," and in the Jaynes'
home it's important...at least to some of us. It was
Friday night, and my family and I were rooting for
the University of North Carolina Tar Heels as they
took on Southern California in the NCAA basketball tournament. All three of us had graduated from
UNC, and it wasn't looking too good for the home
team. By the end of the first half, we were behind
by 16 points.

"We're going to lose," we agreed.

"It's not worth staying up for," Steve said. "It's late,
I'm tired, and they look tired too. I don't want to
watch them get creamed. They'll never come back—
down 16 points!"

So we turned off the television and said our good-nights.

You can imagine our surprise Saturday morning when we opened the newspaper to read the headline: "It's a Tar Heel Blitz!" They had come from behind to win the game 74-64…and we missed it.

I could almost hear God in the background teasing me. *See, you quit too soon…again.*

Sometimes when we're struggling in life and it looks like we're going to lose, we turn off the game and go to bed. But just because it looks like we're losing doesn't mean we are. The game's not over! God is still at work, and if we give up, we'll miss the thrill of victory. And I don't know about you, but I don't want to hear about it secondhand or miss a single second of the miraculous win.

130

The Lighthouse

She watches over the affairs of her household.
PROVERBS 31:27

There she stood, this landmark of the rugged North Carolina coast. The Cape Hatteras Lighthouse, built in 1870, served as sentinel to thousands of sailors who made their way through the "Graveyard of the Atlantic." And now this fair lady was in danger. Through the years strong tides and shifting winds had eroded the coastline, leaving the lighthouse only 120 feet from the encroaching sea. At high tide waves licked at her foundation and taunted her sure footing, threatening to topple her into the sea.

After years of angry debate, several scientific studies, and potential lawsuits, a decision was made to move this beloved landmark. Twenty-three days after the tedious journey began, the Cape Hatteras Lighthouse reached the end of its 2,900 foot trek and now rests 1,600 feet from the water's edge.

Safe for 100 more years.

I looked at the lighthouse and wondered, *Why were the residents so passionate about the lighthouse's destiny? Why would Congress give $10 million to save it?*

And a still, small voice answered, *Because some landmarks are worth fighting for.*

I have always seen a strong resemblance between beacons that watch over the sea and mothers who watch over their tiny fleets. A mother is a beacon who watches over her family, pointing them out to sea and welcoming them to the safe harbor of home.

As I considered the efforts that went into moving the lighthouse, my heart stirred with the importance of motherhood and the God-given roles and responsibilities we have to shine the light of Christ along the rugged shoreline of life.

Some landmarks are worth fighting for, and the importance of motherhood is one of them.

131

Prayer Is a Two-Way Street

He wakens me morning by morning,
wakens my ear to listen like one being taught.

ISAIAH 50:4

A hurricane was coming, and I was trapped in evacuation traffic as I headed toward our home near Charlotte. Rain pelted my windshield and trees swayed in the gusty wind as I joined several thousand travelers trying to outrun the storm. The lanes headed west from the coast were clogged arteries, but only a few brave souls dared to travel in the opposite direction.

During my adventure God and I had plenty of time for conversation. He showed me that my journey home was a picture of a typical prayer life. In one lane were panicky people as far as the eye could see, just as a long line of people are always calling out to God for help. But the eastbound lane depicted the scant few who actually listen when they pray.

While prayer should be a two-way street, many of us spend far more time in the emergency lane directing our prayers to God, and far too little time in the listening lane waiting for His direction. But I have learned that what God has to say to me is far more important than what I have to say to Him, and I need to be praying in both lanes—speaking *and* listening.

I made it home just as the hurricane hit full force. I listened to the whistling wind, the shattering trees, and my heavenly Father, who whispered a reminder that His name is a strong tower. The righteous run to it and are safe.

132

Heavenly Perspective

The city [the new Jerusalem] does not need the
sun or the moon to shine on it, for the glory of
God gives it light, and the Lamb is its lamp.

REVELATION 21:23

Steve woke one morning with a nostalgic urge to revisit the small town where he spent his first eight years of life. I had heard endless stories of his brother and him playing kick-the-can and baseball in their front yard, which was "at least the size of a football field." The long hardwood hallway in their spacious home, where they slid sock-footed, was "at least as long as a bowling alley." They boasted of huge grassy hills where they rolled down laughing and itching all the way.

However, when he pulled up to the marked spot on his treasure map that day, he blinked in disbelief. The "spacious" home was a small bungalow, the "football field size" front yard was a mere square of grass, and the "rolling hills" were no more than two humps in the ground. As he drove past each landmark, Steve kept saying, "Everything is so much smaller than I remember."

As I listened to my husband recount his adventure, my mind wandered heavenward. To us, God's children, our world seems so grand with majestic sunsets, an endless expanse of stars, and vast rolling seas. However, when we arrive in heaven to spend eternity with God, we'll see just how small our world truly was. And the earth's beauty will pale in comparison to the majestic glory that God has waiting for us just around the bend.

133

Eyes that Cannot See

*I am the light of the world. Whoever follows me will
never walk in darkness, but will have the light of life.*

The cave was dark and dank. The sign read "Linville Caverns," but as I suspected, cavern was just a nice name for cave. Like three explorers, my husband, son, and I followed a tour guide as we slipped into a world of darkness. The guide held a small flashlight to point the way down the slippery path and draw our attention to sleeping bats, sudden drop-offs, and dripping stalactites.

Deep into the throat of the cave, the guide turned off the flashlight.

"This is the closest you'll ever get to total darkness," he said.

It was dark. Very dark. I wanted to escape, but the guide was the only one with the light, and we were at his mercy.

After a few moments he turned the flashlight on, and we started our journey back toward the opening of the cave. On the way out I noticed an underground stream full of large fish swimming erratically and bumping into each other.

"There's something strange about those fish," I said to the guide. "What's wrong with them?"

"Those fish have never seen the light of day," he said. "Because of the darkness, they're all blind. They have eyes, but they can't see."

As we emerged from our tour of darkness, I was thankful for the bright light that welcomed our return. Then I realized that God had been on the tour with us and had used the blind fish to remind me what walking in spiritual darkness can do—eventually make us blind. But when we walk in the light of Christ, our eyes are open. We stop living erratically but flow in the current of God's amazing love.

134

Divine Appointment

Jesus said, "Take care of my sheep."

JOHN 21:16

A beautiful young woman stumbled into the airplane obviously exhausted. She was dressed in skintight jeans, a distracting, low-cut T-shirt, and sunglasses that hid something…but I wasn't sure what.

"They messed up my ticket, and I don't have a seat," she complained to the flight attendant.

"This one's empty," I offered, pointing to the seat next to me.

I pulled out my book *Your Scars Are Beautiful to God* to prepare for an upcoming interview, but I sensed God saying, *Put down the book and talk to this girl.*

God, she doesn't want to talk, I argued.

Put down the book and talk to this girl.

I put down the book and turned to my fellow passenger.

"Where are you headed?" I asked.

"Home."

"Where's home?"

"A small town I'm sure you've never heard of." Then she glanced down at the book in my lap. "Scars. Well, I've certainly got a lot of those."

"So do I," I said. "That's why I wrote the book."

"You wrote it?" She was surprised.

For the next hour and a half, this young girl poured out her heart to me. She had been abandoned, sexually abused, and misused. My heart broke as she told me story after story of cruelties that had been done to her mingled with bad choices made through her. I held Beth's hand, and God's sorrow filled my heart. As I prayed for her, tears spilled down her cheeks to wash away the years of regret.

We parted ways, but the memory lingered. God allowed me to apply His healing salve to the wounds of one of His little lambs.

There was no mix-up in her airline ticket; she had a divine seat assignment made by God.

135

Backside of the Island

Why are you downcast, O my soul?
Why so disturbed within me?
Put your hope in God,
for I will yet praise him,
my Savior and my God.

PSALM 42:11

The cruise ship docked at Cozumel Island. Steve and I walked down the ramp and into the hustle and bustle of locals waiting to entertain the new batch of tourists entering their bit of paradise. We rented a small motorcycle, donned our helmets, and set out on an adventure to circle the perimeter of the island. It wasn't too long before civilization lay behind us and the open road promised romantic scenery.

But after several miles, the landscape of pristine, white sandy beaches changed. Lush palms transformed into bare craggy branches, seagulls were replaced with dark, menacing vultures, and the terrain was piled high with debris. We were lone travelers on the backside of the island, and we suddenly realized we were unprotected prey for any number of predators watching for unsuspecting tourists who lost their way. The stench of the island landfill assaulted our senses and circling birds seemed to be waiting for our demise.

"Can't this thing go any faster?" I asked.

"It's wide open," Steve said.

Three hours later we were back on the boat, still shaking from our experience.

After thinking about our trip from paradise to the landfill and back again, I saw a resemblance to life. Sometimes I feel as if I'm on the backside of the island. I look around and see garbage all around me. I sense vultures circling, waiting for me to fall so they can pick me apart.

"Get me out of here!" I cry to God.

Keep going, He says. *Don't stop! Press on!*

We weren't made for the garbage heap, and when we press on through those difficult days, we'll be back in paradise before we know it.

136

For as Long as We Both Shall Live

*For this reason a man will leave his
father and mother and be united to his
wife, and they will become one flesh.*

*F*aces lined with years embraced cheek to cheek. Weathered hands and arthritic fingers intertwined. Slow but steady gaits served as a picture of enduring love in the winter of their lives. We were gathered to celebrate my in-laws' sixtieth wedding anniversary. Like a rare treasure, their legacy of commitment and enduring love is the inheritance they leave to four grown children, five grown grandchildren, and a growing number of great-grandchildren.

Bruce and Mary Ellen were childhood sweethearts who grew up in the mountains of North Carolina. They were a striking couple in their day. His muscular build, 32-inch waist, and 6'4" stature towered over Mary Ellen's 5'3" frame with curves in all the right places. No one was surprised when Bruce asked Mary Ellen to be his bride just a few days after her graduation. On a beautiful fall day in 1943 they became husband and wife. When they said the words, "till death do us part," they meant it. It was a vow made to one another and to God, and the thought of anything other than a lifelong commitment was inconceivable...no matter what.

I sat across the table from this amazing couple and watched as Mary Ellen lovingly wiped something from her husband's face. I saw tears pool in his eyes when he spoke about his bride. And though the years have changed their bodies, they are still a striking couple. Two ordinary people, serving an extraordinary God, offering us a rare and beautiful portrait of a marriage that lasts a lifetime.

137

Jesus Loves Me

Whoever does not love does not know God, because God is love.

1 JOHN 4:8

It was the first anniversary of the terrorist attacks of September 11, 2001. The rubble from the World Trade Centers had been cleared and the Pentagon repaired, but men and women all across America still mourned the 3,000 lives lost on that dark day. In my hometown a memorial was set up on an expanse of land with a sea of 12-inch white crosses representing the men and women who died.

Kathy went to see the memorial with her daughter and three-year-old niece, Taylor. It was difficult for young Taylor to understand what was going on and why so many people were sad, but she obediently walked hand in hand with her cousin between the tiny crosses. At some point, little Taylor wandered away from her family.

It was reverently silent as the crowd of mourners looked at the names inscribed on the white memorials.

Then, as if coming directly from heaven, a small voice could be heard floating on the breeze. Everyone turned to notice a little girl with outstretched arms twirling in circles among the crosses. With face lifted toward the sky, she sang:

> Jesus loves me, this I know,
> For the Bible tells me so.
> Little ones to Him belong,
> They are weak but He is strong.
> Yes, Jesus loves me.
> Yes, Jesus loves me.
> Yes, Jesus loves me.
> The Bible tells me so.

Time stood still as hundreds of mourners turned their attention to one small girl with a big message. Even in the midst of pain, with the loss of life and broken dreams, Jesus still loves us.

138

A Tough Cookie Crumbles

*It is by grace you have been saved, through
faith—and this not from yourselves, it is the gift
of God—not by works, so that no one can boast.*

EPHESIANS 2:8-9

Allan was a tough cookie. He didn't drink every day, but when he did, he usually got drunk and terrorized his household. On many occasions his outbursts resulted in shattered furniture, a battered wife, and terrified children.

But something happened in his home that began a domino of miracles. His 14-year-old daughter turned her life over to Jesus Christ. God's presence infiltrated their home and began to tenderize Allan's tough heart.

Though Allan heard the gospel, he felt he'd done too many horrible things to be forgiven. He couldn't understand God's grace or believe it was available to him.

Five years after his daughter's commitment to Christ, Allan was on the verge of a nervous breakdown.

Hundreds of miles from home he searched out a pastor who was physically building a church in the woods.

"What can I do for you?" the preacher asked.

"I need help," Allan said.

For the next few hours Allan poured out his heart to this stranger and told him everything he'd ever done. Then the preacher put his arm around Allan and said, "Now, Allan, let me tell you my story."

Allan finally understood God's grace on that hot July day in the woods of Pennsylvania, and he accepted Jesus as his Savior. He'd met a man who was not ashamed of the scars in his own life and saw the grace and forgiveness of Christ displayed in a life that mirrored his own.

"I knew that if Jesus could forgive that man and he could be a preacher," Allan said later, "then He could forgive me too."

Allan was my dad.

An Invitation

As you've read about the "God-sightings" in my life, I'm sure God has reminded you of the many times He's turned your ordinary days into extraordinary moments. Now that we're friends, I'd love to hear your stories! Dust for God's fingerprints, log onto **www.extraordinarymomentswithGod.com**, and tell me how you've seen God's presence in your life. While you're there, read the stories of men and women from around the world. I hope they inspire and encourage your life with God.

YOUR SCARS ARE BEAUTIFUL TO GOD
Finding Peace and Purpose in the Hurts of Your Past

Physical scars represent a story, a moment in your life, and they show others there is a history and a healing. Your internal scars—invisible marks from heartbreak, mistakes, and losses—also represent stories of healing and restoration. Author Sharon Jaynes' gentle insight will help you give your wounds 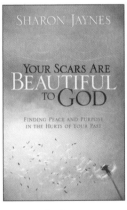 to the One who sees your beauty and who can turn pain into purpose and heartache into hope as you…

- recognize Jesus through your scars
- remove the mask and be real
- release the power of healed wounds

Includes a Bible study guide for personal or group use.

BECOMING THE WOMAN OF HIS DREAMS

Seven Qualities Every Man Longs For

Do you want to become the woman of your husband's dreams? The woman who makes him sorry to leave in the morning and eager to come home at night? If you would like a little "wow!" back in your relationship with the man you married, *Becoming the Woman of His Dreams* offers you an insightful look at the won-

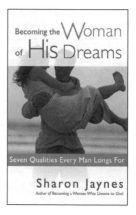

derful, unique, and God-ordained role only you have in your husband's life.

Includes a Bible study guide for personal or group use.

BUILDING AN EFFECTIVE WOMEN'S MINISTRY
Develop a Plan • Gather a Team • Watch God Work

Do you want to develop or improve a women's ministry but feel overwhelmed by the responsibility? Uncertain about where to start? Sharon Jaynes, vice president of Proverbs 31 Ministries, provides clear answers to nearly any question you can think of and presents the planning tools and confidence-builders 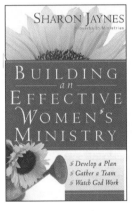 you need to succeed. Discover how to identify your ministry's mission; develop a leadership team; avoid burnout and achieve balance; create programs that nurture, reach out, and revive; and much more!

The Power of a Woman's Words

"You have incredible power in your sphere of influence with the words you speak!" says popular speaker Sharon Jaynes. Words are one of the most powerful forces in the universe, and they can be used for good or evil.

Our words have the power to build courage into a husband's life, instill confidence into a child's heart, fan into flames a friend's smoldering dreams, and draw the lost to Christ.

Do you desire to use your words to build up, encourage, and cheer? Do you want to have more control over that mighty force called the tongue? Then this book is for you!

An easy-to-use workbook and study guide, perfect for individual or group study, is also available.

EXPERIENCE THE ULTIMATE MAKEOVER
Discovering God's Transforming Power

True beauty is not based on external adornments—it's really all about what goes on inside you. In letting God transform your heart, mind, will, and emotions, you'll discover that knowing and loving the supreme Makeover Artist will help you:

- overcome lies you tell yourself and see the truth
- believe that God has a good plan for your life
- leave the past in the past and find peace in the present

Sharon gently shares how the "ultimate makeover" is full of promise and possibilities: new beginnings, fresh faith, and the hope of a beauty unique in the universe... the beauty of you.

Includes a Bible study guide for personal or group use.

BECOMING A WOMAN WHO LISTENS TO GOD

Do you long to hear God's voice? Do you have a hard time focusing on Him because of your hectic schedule and demands on your time? Sharon Jaynes understands, and she offers you encouragement and practical help for hearing God's voice daily.

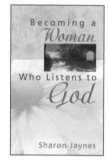

"I discovered that some of God's most memorable messages were delivered while men and women were right in the middle of the hustle and bustle of everyday life," Sharon says. "He spoke to Moses while he was tending sheep, to Gideon while he was threshing wheat, to the woman at the well while she was drawing water for her housework. It's not a matter of does He speak, but will we listen."

More than a how-to book, *Becoming a Woman Who Listens to God* is a warm, fun, tender look at recognizing the wonderful and unexpected ways God reaches out to you with His love and presence.